1 MONTH OF
FREE
READING

at
www.ForgottenBooks.com

By purchasing this book you are eligible for one month membership to ForgottenBooks.com, giving you unlimited access to our entire collection of over 1,000,000 titles via our web site and mobile apps.

To claim your free month visit:

www.forgottenbooks.com/free1374289

ISBN 978-1-397-32776-5
PIBN 11374289

University of Toronto, ON

FACULTY OF MEDICINE.

CALENDAR.

SESSION - - 1906-1907.

TORONTO:

THE UNIVERSITY PRESS.

UNIVERSITY OF TORONTO.

Scale of Feet

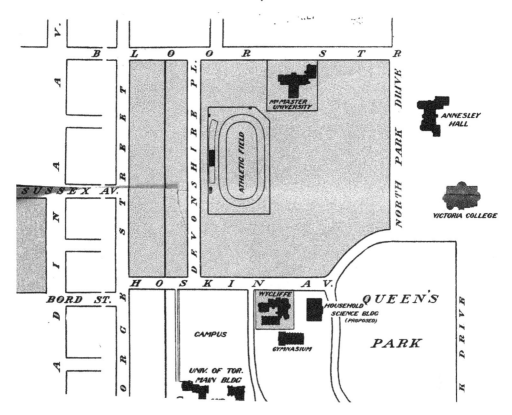

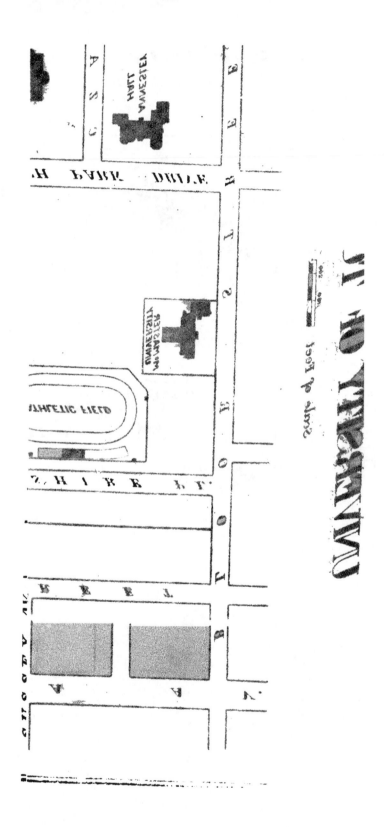

UNIVERSITY OF VERMONT

Scale of Feet 1897

MAIN BUILDI G

University of Toronto

FACULTY OF MEDICINE

CALENDAR

SESSION - - 1906-1907

TORONTO:

THE UNIVERSITY PRESS

University of Toronto.

President: JAMES LOUDON, M.A., LL.D.

Vice-President and Dean of the Faculty of Arts:
R. RAMSAY WRIGHT, M.A., LL.D.

Dean of the Faculty of Medicine:
R. A. REEVE, B.A., M.D., LL.D.

Dean of the Faculty of Applied Science:
JOHN GALBRAITH, M.A., C.E., LL.D.

Registrar: JAMES BREBNER, B.A.

Librarian: HUGH H. LANGTON, M.A.

Curator of the New Museum: H. MONTGOMERY, M.A., B.SC., PH.D.

Bursar: F. A. MOURÉ.

Secretary of the Faculty of Medicine: A. PRIMROSE, M.B., C.M.

Registrar of the Faculty of Applied Science: A. T. LAING, B.A., SC.

Colleges in the Faculty of Arts.

University College.

Principal: MAURICE HUTTON, M.A., LL.D.
Registrar: JAMES BREBNER, B.A.

Victoria College.

President: REV. N. BURWASH, S.T.D., LL.D.
Registrar: A. R. BAIN, M.A., LL.D.

Trinity College.

Provost: REV. T. C. S. MACKLEM, M.A., D.D., LL.D.
Registrar: A. H. YOUNG, M.A.

NOTE.—All communications relating to examinations, curricula, University standing and instruction, are to be addressed to the Registrar of the University, while all correspondence respecting College instruction, residence, etc., is to be addressed to the Registrar of the College concerned.

CALENDAR, 1906.

JANUARY.

S	M	T	W	T	F	S
..	1	2	3	4	5	6
7	8	9	10	11	12	13
14	15	16	17	18	19	20
21	22	23	24	25	26	27
28	29	30	31	..	..	..

FEBRUARY.

S	M	T	W	T	F	S
..	..	..	..	1	2	3
4	5	6	7	8	9	10
11	12	13	14	15	16	17
18	19	20	21	22	23	24
25	26	27	28	..	..	..

MARCH.

S	M	T	W	T	F	S
..	..	..	..	1	2	3
4	5	6	7	8	9	10
11	12	13	14	15	16	17
18	19	20	21	22	23	24
25	26	27	28	29	30	31

APRIL.

S	M	T	W	T	F	S
1	2	3	4	5	6	7
8	9	10	11	12	13	14
15	16	17	18	19	20	21
22	23	24	25	26	27	28
29	30	..	..	..	..	..

MAY.

S	M	T	W	T	F	S
..	..	1	2	3	4	5
6	7	8	9	10	11	12
13	14	15	16	17	18	19
20	21	22	23	24	25	26
27	28	29	30	31	..	..

JUNE.

S	M	T	W	T	F	S
..	..	..	..	..	1	2
3	4	5	6	7	8	9
10	11	12	13	14	15	16
17	18	19	20	21	22	23
24	25	26	27	28	29	30

JULY.

S	M	T	W	T	F	S
1	2	3	4	5	6	7
8	9	10	11	12	13	14
15	16	17	18	19	20	21
22	23	24	25	26	27	28
29	30	31	..	..	..	..

AUGUST.

S	M	T	W	T	F	S
..	..	..	1	2	3	4
5	6	7	8	9	10	11
12	13	14	15	16	17	18
19	20	21	22	23	24	25
26	27	28	29	30	31	..

SEPTEMBER.

S	M	T	W	T	F	S
..	..	..	..	..	..	1
2	3	4	5	6	7	8
9	10	11	12	13	14	15
16	17	18	19	20	21	22
23	24	25	26	27	28	29
30	..	..	..	..	..	..

OCTOBER.

S	M	T	W	T	F	S
..	1	2	3	4	5	6
7	8	9	10	11	12	13
14	15	16	17	18	19	20
21	22	23	24	25	26	27
28	29	30	31	..	..	..

NOVEMBER.

S	M	T	W	T	F	S
..	..	..	..	1	2	3
4	5	6	7	8	9	10
11	12	13	14	15	16	17
18	19	20	21	22	23	24
25	26	27	28	29	30	..

DECEMBER.

S	M	T	W	T	F	S
..	..	..	..	..	..	1
2	3	4	5	6	7	8
9	10	11	12	13	14	15
16	17	18	19	20	21	22
23	24	25	26	27	28	29
30	31	..	..	..	..	..

CALENDAR, 1907.

JANUARY.

S	M	T	W	T	F	S
..	..	1	2	3	4	5
6	7	8	9	10	11	12
13	14	15	16	17	18	19
20	21	22	23	24	25	26
27	28	29	30	31	..	..

FEBRUARY.

S	M	T	W	T	F	S
..	..	..	..	..	1	2
3	4	5	6	7	8	9
10	11	12	13	14	15	16
17	18	19	20	21	22	23
24	25	26	27	28	..	..

MARCH.

S	M	T	W	T	F	S
..	..	..	..	..	1	2
3	4	5	6	7	8	9
10	11	12	13	14	15	16
17	18	19	20	21	22	23
24	25	26	27	28	29	30
31	..	..	..	..	..	..

APRIL.

S	M	T	W	T	F	S
..	1	2	3	4	5	6
7	8	9	10	11	12	13
14	15	16	17	18	19	20
21	22	23	24	25	26	27
28	29	30	..	..	..	..

MAY.

S	M	T	W	T	F	S
..	..	..	1	2	3	4
5	6	7	8	9	10	11
12	13	14	15	16	17	18
19	20	21	22	23	24	25
26	27	28	29	30	31	..

JUNE.

S	M	T	W	T	F	S
..	..	..	..	..	..	1
2	3	4	5	6	7	8
9	10	11	12	13	14	15
16	17	18	19	20	21	22
23	24	25	26	27	28	29
30	..	..	..	..	..	..

Meetings of the University Council are held on the last Monday of September, and on the first Monday of other months. Meetings of the Senate are held on the second Friday of October, November, December, January, February and March, on the Friday following Easter Sunday, and on the Wednesday preceding Commencement in June. Meetings of the Faculty of Medicine are held on the second Friday of the month, from October to May, inclusive.

1906—Sept. 12—Supplemental Examinations in all Faculties begin.

Sept. 15—Registration of Students in Arts by the Registrar, and in Medicine by the Secretary of the Medical Faculty.

Sept. 26—Supplemental Examinations in Dentistry begin.

Oct. 1—Academic year begins; enrolment in classes by the various Professors.

Dec. 11—Local Examinations in Music begin.

Dec. 18-21—Term Examinations.

Dec. 21—Michaelmas Term ends.

Dec. 25—University Buildings closed.

1907—Jan. 1—University Buildings closed.

Jan. 7—Easter Term begins.

Feb. 12—Faculty Dinner.

Feb. 13—University Buildings closed.

March 29—University Buildings closed.

March 31—Last day for presentation of LL.B. and B.A.Sc. theses.

April 1—Last day for the presentation of M.A. theses.

April 8—Annual Meeting of Faculty of Medicine.

April 13—Annual Examinations in Applied Science and Engineering begin.

April 15—Annual Examinations in Dentistry begin.

April 17-19—Term Examinations.

April 19—Lectures in Arts end.

May 1—Annual Examinations in Arts, Law, Medicine, Pharmacy, Music and Agriculture begin.

" Applications for the Alexander Mackenzie Fellowships in Political Science.

May 20—Medical session ends.

May 24—University Buildings closed.

" Last day for giving notice of candidature for Matriculation Scholarships.

June 1—Applications for Fellowships.

June 4—Local Examinations in Music begin.

June 7—University Commencement.

June 12—Junior and Senior Matriculation at centres outside the Province of Ontario.

" Senior Matriculation Examination in Arts begins.

July 1—University Buildings closed.

N.B.—Candidates are required to give notice to the Registrar of intention to present themselves at the annual examinations in Arts and Medicine on or before March 15th. At the examination for Matriculation Scholarships similar notice must be given on or before the 24th May, and at any other University examination at least three weeks before the commencement of the examination.

The University of Toronto.

FACULTY OF ARTS.
1905-1906.

President . . . . JAMES LOUDON, M.A., LL.D.
Vice-President and Dean of the Faculty . . . . . R. RAMSAY WRIGHT, M.A., B.Sc., LL.D.
Registrar . . . . JAMES BREBNER, B.A.
Librarian . . . . HUGH H. LANGTON, M.A.
Bursar . . . . F. A. MOURÉ, ESQ.

A. H. ABBOTT, B.A., PH.D., *Assistant in Psychological Laboratory and Lecturer in Philosophy.*   46 Howland Avenue.

F. B. ALLAN, M.A., PH.D., *Lecturer in Chemistry.*
370 Brunswick Avenue.

MISS F. M. ASHALL, *Class Assistant in Physics.*   33 Seaton Street.

ALFRED BAKER, M.A., *Professor of Mathematics.*   81 Madison Avenue.

F. L. BARBER, M.A., *Class Assistant in the Psychological Laboratory.*
33 Bloor Street East.

B. A. BENSLEY, B.A., PH.D., *Lecturer in Zoology and Assistant Curator of the Biological Museum.*   73 Grosvenor Street.

MISS C. C. BENSON, B.A., PH.D., *Demonstrator in Physiology for Household Science Students.*   7 Queen's Park.

E. BOYD, B.A., *Lecturer and Laboratory Assistant in Biology.*
119 Bloor Street East.

A. G. BROWN, B.A., *Assistant in Modern History.*   596 Huron Street.

C. A. CHANT, M.A., PH.D., *Lecturer in Physics.*   52 Avenue Road.

R. H. CLARK, B.A., *Junior Assistant in Chemistry.*   8 Irwin Avenue.

E. C. COLE, B.A., *Class Assistant in Biology.*   103 Gloucester Street.

A. P. COLEMAN, M.A., PH.D., *Professor of Geology.*   476 Huron Street.

W. H. CRONYN, B.A., M.B., *Class Assistant in Physiology.*
36 South Drive.

F. J. A. DAVIDSON, B.A., PH.D., *Lecturer in Italian and Spanish.*
22 Madison Avenue.

H. F. DAWES, M.A., *Assistant Demonstrator in Physics.*
201 McCaul Street.

J. A. M. DAWSON, B.A., *Junior Assistant in Chemistry.*

234 Brunswick Avenue.

A. T. DE LUBY, M.A., *Associate Professor of Mathematics.*

110 Bedford Road.

J. S DE LURY, B.A., *Assistant in Mineralogy.*   110 Bedford Road.

R. E. DE LURY, B.A., *Fellow in Chemistry.*   110 Bedford Road.

D. DIX, M.A., *Class Assistant in the Psychological Laboratory.*

Knox College.

J. H. FAULL, B.A., PH.D., *Lecturer in Botany.*   102 Yorkville Avenue.

E. FIDLAR, B.A., *Assistant Demonstrator in Physiology.* 16 Wood Street.

J. C. FIELDS, B.A., PH.D., *Associate Professor of Mathematics.*

60 Sussex Avenue.

E. L. C. FORSTER, B.A., *Assistant in Chemistry.*   83 College Street.

W. H. FRASER, M.A., *Professor of Italian and Spanish.*

67 Madison Avenue.

C. A. FRENCH, *Class Assistant in Physics.*   128 D'Arcy Street.

J. A. GARDINER, *Class Assistant in Physics.*   18½ Nassau Street.

D. A. L. GRAHAM, M.B., *Assistant Demonstrator in Physiology.*

New Medical Building.

J. S. GRAHAM, M.B., *Class Assistant in Physiology.*

55 College Street.

G. C. GRAY, *Class Assistant in Physiology.*

50 Ann Street.

W. B. HAMILTON, *Class Assistant in Physics.*   38 Collier Street.

A. HENDERSON, B.A., *Class Assistant in Physiology.*

46 Homewood Avenue.

E. M. HENDERSON, B.A., *Class Assistant in Physiology.*

155 Crescent Road.

V. E. HENDERSON, M.A., M.B., *Demonstrator in Physiology.*

155 Crescent Road.

A. C. HENDRICK, M.A., M.B., *Assistant Demonstrator in Physiology.*

323 College Street.

C. M. HINCKS, B.A., *Class Assistant in Biology.*   225 Dunn Avenue.

R. E. HORE, B.A., *Assistant in Mineralogy.*   108 Hazelton Avenue.

W. HOUSTON, M.A., *Special Lecturer in Canadian Constitutional History.*

164 Walmer Road.

J. G. HUME, M.A., PH.D., *Professor of History of Philosophy.*

58 Spadina Road.

A. G. HUNTSMAN, B.A., *Class Assistant in Biology.*

255 Gerrard Street East.

MAURICE HUTTON, M.A., LL.D., *Professor of Comparative Philology.*

University College.

MISS M. JANSEN, PH.D., *Class Assistant in the Psychological Laboratory.* . . . . . .   81 Robert Street.

W. C. JAQUES, B.A., *Lecture Assistant in Physics.*
16 St. Joseph Street.

A. E. JOHNS, *Class Assistant in Physics.*   69 Robert Street.

MISS L. B. JOHNSON, M.A., *Assistant Demonstrator in Physics.*
69 Sussex Avenue.

F. B. KENRICK, M.A., PH.D., *Lecturer in Chemistry.*   209 John Street.

A. KIRSCHMANN, M.A., PH.D., *Professor of Philosophy and Director of the Psychological Laboratory.*   54 St. George Street.

E. J. KYLIE, B.A., *Lecturer in Modern History.*   40 Roxborough Street.

W. R. LANG, D.SC., *Professor of Chemistry and Director of Chemical Department.*   8 University Crescent.

W. B. LARGE, *Assistant Demonstrator in Physiology.*   3 Queen's Park.

A. H. F. LEFROY, M.A., *Professor of Roman Law and Jurisprudence.*
Clinton Avenue, Deer Park.

JAMES LOUDON, M.A., LL.D., *Professor of Physics.*
83 St. George Street.

W. J. LOUDON, B.A., *Associate Professor of Physics.*   133 Walmer Road.

A. B. MACALLUM, M.A., M.B., PH.D., *Professor of Physiology.*
59 St. George Street.

E. A. McCULLOCH, B.A., M.B., *Class Assistant in Biology.*
167 College Street.

A. J. MACKENZIE, B.A., M.B., LL.B., *Class Assistant in Biology.*
154 Carlton Street.

M. A. MACKENZIE, M.A., *Associate Professor of Mathematics.*
1 Bellwoods Park.

M. D. McKICHAN, B.A., M.B., *Class Assistant in Biology.*
Broadview Avenue and Danforth Road.

J. MACLACHLAN, *Assistant Demonstrator in Physiology.*
152 Walmer Road.

J. R. McLEAN, M.A., *Lecturer in Public Speaking.*   121 Carlton Street.

S. J. McLEAN, M.A., PH.D., *Associate Professor of Political Economy.*

J. C. McLENNAN, B.A., PH.D., *Associate Professor of Physics and Director of the Physical Laboratory.*   The Dean's House.

W. F. McPHEDRAN, B.A., *Class Assistant in Physiology.*
151 Bloor Street West.

J. MAVOR, *Professor of Political Economy.*   8 University Crescent.

F. D. MEADER, B.A., *Assistant Demonstrator in Physics.*
502½ Yonge Street.

MISS M. L. MENTEN, B.A., *Class Assistant in Physiology.*
7 Queen's Park.

F. R. MILLER, B.A., *Assistant Demonstrator in Physiology.*
28 Carlton Street.

W. L. MILLER, B.A., PH.D., *Associate Professor of Chemistry.*
50 St. Albans Street.

J. G. PARKER, B.A., *Fellow in Mathematics.*　104 Bernard Avenue.

W. A. PARKS, B.A., PH.D., *Associate Professor of Geology.*
69 Albany Avenue.

W. H. PIERSOL, B.A., M.B., *Lecturer in Elementary Biology and Histology.*　26 Albany Avenue.

J. K. ROBERTSON, *Class Assistant in Physics.*　8 Division Street.

T. R. ROBINSON, M.A., *Special Lecturer in Philosophy.*
43 Gore Vale Avenue.

WALLACE SCOTT, B.A., M.B., *Class Assistant in Biology.*
576 Church Street.

W. G. SMITH, B.A., *Assistant in Psychological Laboratory and Special
Lecturer in Philosophy.*　Howland Avenue.

MISS M. K. STRONG, B.A., *Class Assistant in Psychological Laboratory.*

MISS B. TAMBLYN, *Instructor in Household Science.*　12 Irwin Avenue.

R. B. THOMSON, B.A., *Instructor in Botany.*　34 Henry Street.

R. B. STEWART, B.A., *Junior Assistant in Chemistry.*　175 McCaul Street.

F. TRACY, B.A., PH.D., *Lecturer in Philosophy.*　173 Walmer Road.

T. L. WALKER, M.A., PH.D., *Professor of Mineralogy and Petrography.*
Alexandra Apartments.

MISS E. J. WILLIAMS, *Class Assistant in Physics.*　Annesley Hall.

W. WILSON, B.A., *Class Assistant in Biology.*　75 Grosvenor Street.

C. WOODHOUSE, *Class Assistant in Physics.*　58 Duke Street.

R. RAMSAY WRIGHT, M.A., B.SC., LL.D., *Professor of Biology.*
St. George Apartments.

G. M. WRONG, M.A., *Professor of Modern History.*　467 Jarvis Street.

J. McGREGOR YOUNG, M.A., *Professor of Constitutional and International
Law and Constitutional History.*　The Dean's House.

UNIVERSITY COLLEGE.
1905-1906.

Principal..........................MAURICE HUTTON, M.A., LL.D.

Registrar...............................JAMES BREBNER, B.A.

W. J. ALEXANDER, B.A., PH.D., *Professor of English.* 110 Avenue Road.

A. G. BROWN, B.A., *Temporary Lecturer in Ancient History and Latin.*
596 Huron Street.

J. H. CAMERON, M.A., *Associate Professor of French.*
476 Huron Street.

A. CARRUTHERS, M.A., *Associate Professor of Greek Literature and*
Archæology. 132 Tyndall Avenue.

SAINT-ELME DE CHAMP, B. ÈS L., (Officier d'Académie), *Instructor in*
French. 301 Jarvis Street.

T. EAKIN, M.A., PH.D., *Lecturer in Oriental Languages.*
587 Spadina Avenue.

J. FLETCHER, M.A., LL.D., *Professor of Latin.* 532 Huron Street.

J. G. HUME, M.A., PH.D., *Professor of Ethics.* 58 Spadina Road.

MAURICE HUTTON, M.A., LL.D., *Professor of Greek.* University College.

G. W. JOHNSTON, B.A., PH.D., *Lecturer in Latin.* 129 Walmer Road.

D. R. KEYS, M.A., *Associate Professor of Anglo-Saxon.*
87 Avenue Road.

J. F. McCURDY, PH.D., LL.D., *Professor of Oriental Literature.*
72 Spadina Road.

C. A. McRAE, M.A., *Instructor in Oriental Languages.*
598 College Street.

W. S. MILNER, M.A., *Associate Professor of Latin and Ancient History.*
19 Albany Avenue.

G. H. NEEDLER, B.A., PH.D., *Associate Professor of German.*
103 Bedford Road.

J. SQUAIR, B.A., *Professor of French.* 61 Major Street.

W. H. TACKABERRY, M.A., *Instructor in Greek.* 116 Albany Avenue.

P. TOEWS, M.A., PH.D., *Instructor in German.* 60 Czar Street.

W. H. VAN DER SMISSEN, M.A., *Professor of German.* 15 Surrey Place.

M. W. WALLACE, B.A., PH.D., *Lecturer in English.* 69 Harbord Street.

VICTORIA COLLEGE—FACULTY OF ARTS.

1905-1906.

President .... Rev. N. Burwash, S.T.D., LL.D.
113 Bloor Street West.

Dean .... Rev. A. H. Reynar, M.A., LL.D.

Registrar .... A. R. Bain, M.A., LL.D.

Librarian .... Rev. J. F. McLaughlin, B.A., B.D.

Secretary .... J. C. Robertson, M.A.

Co-Treasurers .... Hon. G. A. Cox, Rev. John Potts, D.D.

Miss M. E. T. Addison, B.A., *Lecturer in German.* Annesley Hall.

Rev. W. T. Allison, M.A., *Lecturer in Rhetoric and English Composition.* Stayner.

Rev. E. I. Badgley, M.A., LL.D. (*Obit.*)
Egerton Ryerson Professor of Mental and Moral Philosophy.

A. R. Bain, M.A., LL.D., *Nelles Professor of Ancient History.*
Victoria College.

A. J. Bell, M.A., Ph.D., *Macdonald Professor of the Latin Language and Literature.* 17 Avenue Road.

Rev. J. Burwash, M.A., D.Sc., LL.D., *Professor of English Bible.*
89 Avenue Road.

Pelham Edgar, Ph.D., *Professor of the French Language and Literature.* 21 Elgin Avenue.

L. E. Horning, M.A., Ph.D., *Professor of Teutonic Philology.*
Victoria College.

A. E. Lang, M.A., *Professor of the German Language and Literature.*
104 Spadina Road.

A. L. Langford, M.A., *Associate Professor of the Greek Language and Literature.* 119 Farnham Avenue.

Rev. J. F. McLaughlin, B.A., B.D., *Professor of Oriental Languages and Literature.* 30 Bernard Avenue.

E. Masson, *Instructor in French.* (*Obit.*)

Rev. Austin P. Misener, M.A., B.D., *Lecturer in Oriental Languages and Literature.* 105 Yorkville Avenue.

Rev. Alfred H. Reynar, M.A., LL.D., *William Gooderham Professor of English Literature.* Victoria College.

J. C. Robertson, M.A., *Professor of the Greek Language and Philosophy.*
115 Spadina Road.

J. H. Shepherd, *Instructor in Elocution.* Weston.

Rev. F. H. Wallace, M.A., D.D., *George A. Cox Professor of Biblical Greek.* 95 Bedford Road.

TRINITY COLLEGE—FACULTY OF ARTS.
1905-1906.

Provost and Dean of the Faculty of Divinity,
Rev. T. C. Street Macklem, M.A., D.D., LL.D.

Dean of Residence...................Rev. H. T. F. Duckworth, M.A.

Registrar.......................................A. H. Young, M.A.

Librarian..............................G. Oswald Smith, M.A.

Bursar.........................Rev. William Jones, M.A., D.C.L.

J. W. G. Andras, Ph.D. (Tuebingen), of the Inner Temple, *Lecturer in French.*   590 Markham Street.

Rev. E. C. Cayley, M.A., *Special Lecturer in Divinity.*
                    85 Bleecker Street.

Rev. William Clark, F.R.S.C., M.A. (Oxon.), D.D. (Queen's), D.C.L. (Trin.), LL.D. (Hobart), *Professor of Mental and Moral Philosophy and Professor of English Literature.*   Trinity College.

Rev. H. T. F. Duckworth, M.A. (Oxon.), *Professor of Divinity and Lecturer in Classics.*   Trinity College.

Rev. T. H. Hunt, M.A., D.D., *Lecturer in Hebrew and Theology.*
                    Trinity College.

Rev. A. W. Jenks, M.A. (Dartmouth), B.D. (Gen. Theol. Sem. N.Y.), *Professor of Divinity.*   Trinity College.

Rev. William Jones, M.A. (Cantab.), D.C.L. (Trin.), *Emeritus Professor of Mathematics.*   Trinity College.

Rev. C. B. Kenrick, M.A. (Trin.), *Lecturer in Divinity.*
                    209 John Street.

Rev. E. L. King, B.A. (Man.), *Lecturer in Mental Philosophy.*
                    412 Huron Street.

M. A. Mackenzie, A.I.A., M.A. (Trin. and Cantab.), *Professor of Mathematics and Physics.*   1 Bellwoods Park.

H. Montgomery, F.A.A.S., M.A. (Tor.), B.Sc. (Vict.), Ph.D. (Wesleyan, Ill.), *Professor of Natural Science.*   39 Borden Street.

E. T. Owen, M.A. (Trin.), *Lecturer and Fellow in Classics.*
                    Absent on leave.

H. V. Routh, B.A. (Cantab.), *Lecturer in German and Classics.*
                    Trinity College.

E. M. Sait, M.A. (Trin.), *Lecturer in History.*   Trinity College.

H. C. Simpson, B.A. (Oxon.), M.A. (Trin.), *Lecturer in English.*
                    Trinity College.

G. O. Smith, B.A. (Oxon.), M.A. (Trin. and Oxon.), *Professor of Classics.*   229 Crawford Street.

Rev. E. A. Welch, M.A., D.C.L., *Special Lecturer in Divinity.*
                    St. James' Rectory.

A. H. Young, B.A. (Tor.), M.A. (Trin.), *Professor of German.*
                    Trinity College.

UNIVERSITY OF TORONTO—FACULTY OF MEDICINE.
1905-1906.

President..............................JAMES LOUDON, M.A., LL.D.
Dean of Faculty......................R. R. REEVE, B.A., M.D., LL.D.
Registrar........:............................JAMES BREBNER, B.A.
Secretary of the Faculty.................A. PRIMROSE, M.B., C.M.
Busar.........:...................................F. A. MOURÉ, ESQ.

Professores Emeriti.

M. H. AIKINS, B.A., M.D.   J. H. RICHARDSON, M.D.
W. W. OGDEN, M.D.   UZZIEL OGDEN, M.D.

H. W. AIKINS, B.A., M.B., Tor., Associate Professor of Anatomy.
264 Church Street.

F. B. ALLAN, M.A., PH.D., Lecturer in Chemistry.
370 Brunswick Avenue.

J. A. AMYOT, M.B., Tor., Associate Professor of Pathology and Bacteriology.
Thornhill, Ont.

H. B. ANDERSON, M.D., C.M., Trin., Associate Professor in Clinical Medicine.
34 Carlton Street.

T. D. ARCHIBALD, B.A., M.B., Tor., Laboratory Assistant in Bacteriology and Tutor in Medicine.
327 College Street.

A. M. BAINES, M.D., C.M., Trin., Associate Professor of Clinical Medicine and Associate Professor of Pediatries.
228 Bloor Street W.

MISS F. M. ASHALL, Class Assistant in Physics.
33 Seaton Street.

N. H. BEEMER, M.B., Tor., Extra-Mural Professor of Mental Disease.
The Asylum, Mimico.

B. A. BENSLEY, B.A., Tor., PH.D., Col., Lecturer in Zoology.
73 Grosvenor Street.

G. A. BINGHAM, M.B., Tor., M.D., C.M., Trin., Associate Professor of Clinical Surgery and Clinical Anatomy.
68 Isabella Street.

E. C. COLE, B.A., Tor., Class Assistant in Biology.
103 Gloucester Street.

G. BOYD, B.A., M.B., Tor., Associate in Clinical Medicine and in Laryngology and Rhinology.
167 Bloor St. East.

H. A. BRUCE, M.B., Tor., F.R.C.S. Eng., Associate Professor of Clinical Surgery.
64 Bloor Street East.

G. H. BURNHAM, M.D., Tor., F.R.C.S., Edin., Professor of Ophthalmology and Otology.
134 Bloor Street East.

I. H. CAMERON, M.B., Tor., F.R.C.S., Eng., LL.D. Edin., Professor of Surgery and Clinical Sugery.
307 Sherbourne Street.

M H. V. CAMERON, M.B., Tor., Clinical Laboratory Assistant.

W. P. CAVEN, M.B., Tor., Associate Professor of Clinical Medicine.
70 Gerrard Street East.

G. CHAMBERS, B.A., M.B., Tor., Associate in Clinical Medicine.
26 Gerrard Street East.

C. A. CHANT, M.A., PH.D., Lecturer in Physics.
52 Avenue Road.

C. K. CLARKE, M.B., *Extra Mural Professor of Mental Diseases, Asylum for Insane.*   Queen Street West.

F. A. CLARKSON, M.B., Tor., *Assistant Demonstrator in Pathology.*
471 College Street.

R. L. CLARK, B.A., Tor., *Assistant in Chemistry.*   8 Irwin Avenue.

C. J. COPP, M.D.C.M., Trin., *Assistant Demonstrator of Anatomy.*

M. M. CRAWFORD, M.B., Tor., *Assistant Demonstrator in Pathology.*
22 Cottingham Street.

W. H. CRONYN, M.A., M.B., *Assistant Demonstrator in Physiology.*
36 South Drive.

R. E. DELURY, *Fellow in Chemistry*   110 Bedford Road.

J. L. DAVISON, B.A., Tor., M.D., C.M., Trin., *Professor of Clinical Medicine.*   20 Charles Street.

R. J. DWYER, M.B., Tor., M.R.C.P., Lond., *Associate Professor of Clinical Medicine.*   408 Bloor Street West.

J. A. M. DAWSON, B.A., Tor., *Assistant in Chemistry.*
234 Brunswick Avenue.

GEORGE ELLIOTT, M.D., C.M., Trin., *Assistant Demonstrator of Anatomy.*   203 Beverley Street.

W. H. ELLIS, M.A., M.B., Tor., *Professor of Toxicology.*
74 St. Albans Street.

J. H. FAULL, B.A., Tor., *Lecturer in Botany.*   245 McCaul Street.

F. FENTON, M.D., C.M., Trin., *Associate in Clinical Medicine and in Obstetrics.*   75 Bloor Street East.

E. FIDLAR, B.A., *Assistant Demonstrator in Physiology.* 16 Wood Street.

C. A. FRENCH, *Class Assistant in Physics.*   128 D'Arcy Street.

J. T. FOTHERINGHAM, B.A., Tor., M.D., C.M., Trin., *Associate Professor of Medicine and Clinical Medicine.*   20 Wellesley Street.

A. E. JOHNS, *Class Assistant in Physics.*   69 Robert Street.

A. H. GARRATT, M.D., C.M., Trin., *Demonstrator of Clinical Surgery.*
53 College Street.

W. GOLDIE, M.B., Tor., *Associate in Clinical Medicine.*
86 College Street.

A. R. GORDON, M.B., *Associate Professor of Clinical Medicine.*
345 Bloor Street West.

F. LeM. GRASETT, M.B., C.M., Edin., F.R.C.S. Edin., *Professor of Surgery and Clinical Surgery.*   208 Simcoe Street.

JOS. S. GRAHAM, M.B., *Assistant Demonstrator i nPhysiology.*
55 College Street.

G. C. GRAY, *Assistant Demonstrator in Physiology.*   50 Ann Street.

C. M. HINCKS, B.A., Tor., *Class Assistant in Biology.* 225 Dunn Avenue.

A. HENDERSON, B.A., *Assistant Demonstrator in Physiology.*
46 Homewood Avenue.

V. E. HENDERSON, M.A., M.B., Tor., *Demonstrator of Physiology and Pharmacology.*   155 Crescent Road.

A. C. HENDRICK, M.A., M.B., Tor., *Assistant Demonstrator of Anatomy, Class Assistant in Biology and in Physiology.* 323 College Street.

E. R. HOOPER, B.A., M.B., Tor., *Assistant Demonstrator of Anatomy.* 415 Bloor Street West.

G. W. HOWLAND, B.A., M.B., Tor., M.R.C.P., Lond., *Assistant Demonstrator in Pathology and Tutor in Medicine.* 540 Spadina Avenue.

F. B. KENRICK, M.A., Tor., PH.D., Leipsig, *Lecturer in Chemistry.* 209 John Street.

W. B. LARGE, B.Sc., *Assistant Demonstrator in Physiology.* 3 Queen's Park.

W. R. LANG, D.Sc., Glasg., F.I.C., *Professor of Chemistry.* 8 University Crescent.

JAMES LOUDON, M.A., LL.D., Tor., *Professor of Physics.* 83 St. George Street.

J. D. LOUDON, B.A., *Class Assistant in Histology.* 83 St. George Street.

C. P. LUSK, M.D., C.M., Trin., *Demonstrator of Pharmacy.* 99 Bloor Street West.

A. B. MACALLUM, M.A., M.D., Tor., PH.D., Johns Hopkins, F.R.S., *Professor of Physiology.* 59 St. George Street.

J. M. MACCALLUM, B.A., M.D., Tor., *Professor of Materia Medica, Pharmacology and Therapeutics, Associate in Ophthamology and Otology.* 13 Bloor Street West.

W. J. MCCOLLUM, M.B., Tor., *Assistant Demonstrator of Anatomy.* 168 Jarvis Street.

E. A. MCCULLOCH, B.A., Tor., *Class Assistant in Biology.* 203 University Avenue.

G. R. MCDONAGH, M.D., Tor., *Professor of Laryngology and Rhinology.* 140 Carlton Street.

D. MCGILLIVRAY, M.B., Tor., *Assistant Demonstrator in Anatomy and Tutor in Medicine.* 42 Carlton Street.

K. C. MCILWRAITH, M.B., Tor., *Associate in Obstetrics.* 54 Avenue Road.

A. J. MACKENZIE, B.A., LL.B. M.B., Tor., *Assistant Demonstrator of Anatomy and Class Assistant in Histology.* 154 Carlton Street..

J. J. MACKENZIE, B.A., *Professor of Pathology and Bacteriology and Curator of the Museum and Laboratories.* 41 Chestnut Park Rd.

W. MCKEOWN, B.A., M.B., Tor., *Demonstrator in Clinical Surgery.* 7 College Street.

M. D. MCKICHAN, B.A., M.B., *Class Assistant in Biology and Histology.* 10 Withrow Avenue.

J. MACLACHLAN, *Assistant Demonstrator in Physiology.* 152 Walmer Road.

H. M. MCNEIL, B.A., *Class Assistant in Biology.* 69 Beatty Avenue.

A. MCPHEDRAN, M.B., Tor., *Professor of Medicine and Clinical Medicine.* 151 Bloor Street West.

2

W. F. MCPHEDRAN, *Assistant Demonstrator in Physiology.*
151 Bloor Street West.

H. T. MACHELL, M.D., Tor., *Associate Professor of Obstetrics and Pediatrics.*
95 Bellevue Avenue.

J. C. MCLENNAN, B.A., Tor., PH.D., *Associate Professor of Physics Director of the Physical Laboratories.*
The Dean's House.

MISS F. D. MEADER, *Assistant Demonstrator in Physics.*

F. W. MARLOW, M.D., C.M., Trin., F.R.C.S., Eng., *Assistant Demonstrator in Anatomy.*
699 Spadina Avenue.

MISS M. L. MENTEN, B.A., Tor., *Assistant Demonstrator in Physiology.*
Annesley Hall.

J. W. O. MALLOCH, B.A., M.B., Tor., *Assistant Demonstrator of Anatomy, Class Assistant in Physiology.*
237 College Street.

F. R. MILLER, B.A., *Assistant Demonstrator in Physiology.*
280 Carlton Street.

J. C. MITCHELL, M.D., C.M., Trin., *Extra-Mural Professor of Mental Disease.*
Asylum for the Insane, Queen Street West.

W. OLDRIGHT, M.A., M.D., Tor., *Professor of Hygiene and Associate Professor of Clinical Surgery.*
154 Carlton Street.

H. C. PARSONS, B.A., M.D., C.M., Trin., M.R.C.P., Lond., *Associate in Clinical Medicine and Assistant Demonstrator in Pathology.*
72 Bloor Street West.

W. H. PEPLER, M.D., C.M., Trin., *Assistant Demonstrator in Pathology.*
600 Spadina Avenue.

G. A. PETERS, M.B., Tor., F.R.C.S., Eng., *Professor of Surgery and Clinical Surgery.*
102 College Street.

W. H. PIERSOL, B.A., M.D., Tor., *Lecturer in Elementary Biology and Histology.*
26 Albany Avenue.

N. A. POWELL, M.D., C.M., Trin., M.D., Bellevue, N.Y., *Professor of Medical Jurisprudence and Associate Professor of Clinical Surgery.*
167 College Street.

J. K. ROBERTSON, *Class Assistant in Physics.*   8 Division Street.

A. PRIMROSE, M.B., C.M., Edin., *Professor of Anatomy and Director of the Anatomical Department, Associate Professor of Clinical Surgery.*
100 College Street.

R. A. REEVE, B.A., M.D., LL.D., Tor., *Professor of Ophthalmology and Otology.*
48 Bloor Street East.

T. B. RICHARDSON, M.D., C.M., Trin., F.R.C.S., Edin., *Demonstrator in Clinical Surgery.*
128 Bloor Street West.

J. F. W. ROSS, M.B., Tor., *Professor of Gynæcology.*
481 Sherbourne Street.

R. D. RUDOLF, M.D., C.M., Edin., M.R.C.P., Lond., *Associate Professor of Medicine and Associate in Clinical Medicine.*
396 Bloor Street West.

E. S. RYERSON, M.D., C.M., Trin., *Assistant Demonstrator of Anatomy and Pathology.*
216 College Street.

G.S. RYERSON, M.D., C.M., Trin., *Professor of Ophthalmology and Otology.* 66 College Street.

W. A. SCOTT, B.A., M.B., Tor., F.R.C.S., Eng., *Assistant Demonstrator of Anatomy and Class Assistant in Biology.* 576 Church Street.

C. SHEARD, M.D., C.M., Trin., *Professor of Preventive Medicine.*
314 Jarvis Street.

C. B. SHUTTLEWORTH, M.D., C.M., Trin., F.R.C.S., Eng., *Demonstrator of Anatomy and Demonstrator of Clinical Surgery.*
45 Bloor Street East.

G. SILVERTHORN, M.B., Tor., *Demonstrator of Pathology.*
266 College Street.

G. E. SMITH, B.A., M.B., Tor., *Assistant Demonstrator of Anatomy.*
380 King Street West.

F. N. G. STARR, M.B., Tor., *Associate Professor of Clinical Surgery.*
112 College Street.

C. L. STARR, M.B., Tor., *Associate Professor of Clinical Surgery in charge of Orthopœdics.* 224 Bloor Street West.

R. B. STEWART, B.A., Tor., *Assistant in Chemistry.*

W. T. STUART, M.B., Tor., M.D., C.M., Trin., *Associate Professor of Medical Chemistry.* 197 Spadina Avenue.

C. A. TEMPLE, M.D., C.M., Trin., *Demonstrator of Clinical Surgery.*
200 Spadina Avenue.

J. ALGERNON TEMPLE, M.D., C.M., McGill, LL.D., Tor., *Professor of Gynæcology and Operative Obstetrics.* 333 Bloor Street West.

L. TESKEY, M.D., C.M., Trin., *Professor of Surgery and Clinical Surgery.* 612 Spadina Avenue.

W. B. THISTLE, M.D., Tor., *Associate Professor of Clinical Medicine.*
171 College Street.

C. TROW, M.D., C.M., Trin., *Associate Professor in Ophthamology and Otology.* 57 Carlton Street.

C. WOODHOUSE, *Class Assistant in Physics.* 58 Duke Street.

J. F. UREN, M.D., C.M., Trin., *Demonstrator of Clinical Surgery.*
520 Church Street.

H. G. WILSON, B.A., Tor., *Class Assistant in Biology.*

C. J. WAGNER, M.B., Tor., *Demonstrator of Pathology.*
19 Gerrard Street East.

S. H. WESTMAN, M.B., Tor., *Assistant Demonstrator of Anatomy and Class Assistant in Physiology.* 630 Spadina Avenue.

D. J. GIBB WISHART, B.A., Tor., M.D., C.M., McGill, *Associate Professor in Laryngology and Rhinology.* 47 Grosvenor Street.

A. H. WRIGHT, B.A., M.D., Tor., *Professor of Obstetrics.*
30 Gerrard Street East.

R. RAMSAY WRIGHT, M.A., B.Sc., Edin., LL.D., *Professor of Biology.*
St. George Apartments.

MISS E. J. WILLIAMS, *Class Assistant in Physics.* Annesley Hall.

UNIVERSITY OF TORONTO:
FACULTY OF APPLIED SCIENCE AND ENGINEERING.
1905-1906.

President.............JAMES LOUDON, M.A., LL.D.

Dean................JOHN GALBRAITH, M.A., C.E., LL.D.

Registrar............A. T. LAING, B.A.Sc.

. R. ANDERSON, M.A., *Lecturer in Physics.*

. W. ANGUS, B.A.Sc., *Lecturer in Mechanical Engineering.*

. G. R. ARDAGH, B.A.Sc., *Demonstrator in Chemistry.*

. H. ARMOUR, Grad. S.P.S., *Fellow in Electrical Engineering.*

E. B. AYLSWORTH, Grad. S.P.S., *Fellow in Civil Engineering.*

J. W. BAIN, B.A.Sc., *Lecturer in Applied Chemistry.*

M. C. BOSWELL, B.A.Sc., *Demonstrator in Chemistry.*

W. M. BRISTOL, Grad. S.P.S., *Fellow in Drawing.*

J. R. COCKBURN, B.A.Sc., *Lecturer in Drawing.*

A. P. COLEMAN, M.A., PH.D., *Professor of Geology.*

S. R. CRERAR, B.A.Sc., *Fellow in Drawing.*

W. E. DOUGLAS, B.A., *Fellow in Surveying.*

S. DUSHMAN, B.A., *Fellow in Chemistry.*

W. H. ELLIS, M.A., M.B., *Professor of Applied Chemistry.*

J. GALBRAITH, M.A., C.E., LL.D., *Professor of Engineering.*

P. GILLESPIE, B.A.Sc., *Lecturer in Applied Mechanics.*

W. W. GRAY, B.A.Sc., *Fellow in Thermodynamics.*

S. E. McGORMAN, Grad. S.P.S., *Fellow in Mechanical Engineering.*

J. McGOWAN, B.A., B.A.Sc., *Lecturer in Applied Mechanics.*

J. G. McMILLAN, B.A.Sc., *Demonstrator in Mining.*

G. R. MICKLE, B.A., *Professor of Mining.*

L. W. MORDEN, Grad. S.P.S., *Fellow in Physics.*

J. PARKE, B.A.Sc., *Lecture Assistant in Chemistry.*

H. W. PRICE, B.A.Sc., *Lecturer in Electrical Engineering.*

T. R. ROSEBRUGH, M.A., *Professor of Electrical Engineering.*

R. B. ROSS, Grad. S.P.S., *Fellow in Electrical Engineering.*

J. D. SHEPLEY, B.A.Sc., *Fellow in Surveying.*

H. G. SMITH, B.A.Sc., *Fellow in Electrical Engineering.*

L. B. STEWART, O.L.S., D.L.S., *Professor of Surveying and Geodesy.*

C. M. TEASDALE, B.A.Sc., *Fellow in Surveying.*

D. T. TOWNSEND, B.A.Sc., *Fellow in Drawing.*

E. WADE, Grad. S.P.S., *Fellow in Chemistry.*

E. W. WALKER, B.A.Sc., *Fellow in Hydraulics.*

C. H. C. WRIGHT, B.A.Sc., *Professor of Architecture.*

EXAMINERS, 1906.

ARTS.

Classics and Ancient History: A. R. BAIN, M.A., LL.D.; A. J. BELL, M.A., PH.D.; A. CARRUTHERS, M.A.; F. C. COLBECK, B.A.; REV. H. T. F. DUCKWORTH, M.A.; J. FLETCHER, M.A., LL.D.; G. W. JOHNSTON, B.A., PH.D.; A. L. LANGFORD, M.A.; W. S. MILNER, M.A.; J. C. ROBERTSON, M.A.; H. V. ROUTH, B.A.; G. OSWALD SMITH, M.A.; W. H. TACKABERRY, B.A.

English: W. J. ALEXANDER, B.A., PH.D.; W. T. ALLISON, M.A.; W. CLARK, D.C.L.; L. E. HORNING, M.A., PH.D.; D. R. KEYS, M.A.; A. E. LANG, M.A.; A. H. REYNAR, M.A., LL.D.; H. C. SIMPSON, M.A.; M. W. WALLACE, M.A., PH.D.

French: J. W. G. ANDRAS, PH.D.; J. H. CAMERON, M.A.; ST. ELME DE CAMP, B. ès L.; O. P. EDGAR, B.A., PH.D.; H. V. ROUTH, B.A.; J. SQUAIR, B.A.

German: L. E. HORNING, M.A., PH.D.; A. E. LANG, M.A.; G. H. NEEDLER, B.A., PH.D.; P. TOEWS, M.A., PH.D.; W. H. VAN DER SMISSEN, M.A.; A. H. YOUNG, M.A.

Scientific French and German: F. B. KENRICK, M.A., PH.D.; W. A. PARKS, B.A., PH.D.; R. R. WRIGHT, M.A., B.SC., LL.D.

Italian, Spanish and Phonetics: F. J. A. DAVIDSON, M.A., PH.D.; W. H. FRASER, M.A.

Oriental Languages: T. EAKIN, M.A., PH.D.; T. H. HUNT, D.D.; J. F. MCCURDY, PH.D., LL.D.; J. F. MCLAUGHLIN, M.A., B.D.; C. A. MCRAE, M.A.; A. P. MISENER, M.A., B.D.

History and Ethnology: A. G. BROWN, B.A.; E. J. KYLIE, B.A.; E. H. OLIVER, PH.D.; E. M. SAIT, M.A.; G. M. WRONG, M.A.

Political Economy: J. MAVOR; S. J. MCLEAN.

Constitutional History, Law and International Law: W. HOUSTON, M.A.; J. MCGREGOR YOUNG, M.A.

History of English Law, History of Roman Law, Jurisprudence: A. H. F. LEFROY, M.A.

Philosophy: A. H. ABBOTT, B.A., PH.D.; W. CLARK, D.C.L.; J. G. HUME, M.A., PH.D.; E. L. KING, B.A.; A. KIRSCHMANN, PH.D.; T. R. ROBINSON, M.A.; W. G. SMITH, B.A.; F. TRACY, B.A., PH.D.; A. VASCHALDE, D.D.

Mathematics: A. BAKER, M.A.; A. T. DELURY, M.A.; J. C. FIELDS, B.A., PH.D.; M. A. MACKENZIE, M.A.; J. G. PARKER, B.A.

Physics: C. A. CHANT, M.A., PH.D.; J. LOUDON, M.A., LL.D.; W. J. LOUDON, B.A.; M. A. MACKENZIE, M.A.; J. C. MCLENNAN, B.A., PH.D.

Chemistry: F. B. ALLAN, M.A., PH.D.; R. E. DE LURY, B.A.; E. FORSTER, B.A.; F. B. KENRICK, M.A., PH.D.; W. R. LANG, D.SC.; W. L. MILLER, B.A., PH.D.

Biology: B. A. BENSLEY, B.A., PH.D.; E. BOYD, B.A.; J. H. FAULL, B.A., PH.D.; A. G. HUNTSMAN, B.A.; HENRY MONTGOMERY, M.A., PH.D.; W. H. PIERSOL, B.A., M.B.; R. B. THOMSON, B.A.; R. RAMSAY WRIGHT, M.A., B.SC., LL.D.

Physiology: V. E. HENDERSON, M.A., M.B.; A. B. MACALLUM, M.A., M.B., PH.D.

Anatomy: A. PRIMROSE, M.B., C.M.

Mineralogy and Geology: A. P. COLEMAN, M.A., PH.D.; W. A. PARKS, B.A., PH.D.; T. L. WALKER, M.A., PH.D.

World History: W. H. PIERSOL, B.A., M.B.

JUNIOR MATRICULATION.

Classics: G. W. JOHNSTON, B.A., PH.D.; J. McNAUGHTON, M.A.; J. C. ROBERTSON, M.A.

English and History: A. R. BAIN, M.A., LL.D.; E. A. HARDY, B.A.; W. S. W. McLAY, M.A.

French and German: J. W. G. ANDRAS, PH.D.; P. EDGAR, PH.D.; J. SQUAIR, B.A.

Mathematics: W. H. BALLARD, B.A.; J. MATHESON, M.A.; W. PRENDERGAST, B.A.

Science and Geography: F. B. KENRICK, M.A., PH.D.; J. C. McLENNAN, B.A., PH.D.; W. H. PIERSOL, B.A., M.B.

MEDICINE.

M. B. Examiners.

Anatomy: H. W. AIKINS, B.A., M.B.; A. PRIMROSE, M.B., C.M.; C. B. SHUTTLEWORTH, M.D., C.M.

Therapeutics: V. E. HENDERSON, M.A., M.B.

Materia Medica: C. P. LUSK, B.A., M.D.

Medicine and Clinical Medicine: R. D. RUDOLF, M.D., C.M.; J. T. FOTHERINGHAM, B.A., M.B., M.D., C.M.

Surgery and Clinical Surgery: C. L. STARR, M.B.

Obstetrics and Gynæcology: A. BAINES, M.D., C.M.; J. F. W. ROSS, M.B.; J. A. TEMPLE, M.D., C.M.; A. H. WRIGHT, B.A., M.D.

Pathology: J. J. MACKENZIE, B.A.

Ophthalmology and Otology: C. TROW, M.D., C.M.

Laryngology and Rhinology: D. J. GIBB WISHART, B.A., M.D., C.M.

Hygiene: E. E. KITCHEN, M.B.

Medical Jurisprudence: N. A. POWELL, M.D., C.M.

Medical Psychology: N. H. BEEMER, M.B.

Chemistry: F. B. ALLAN, M.A., PH.D.; F. B. KENRICK, M.A., PH.D.;
W. R. LANG, D.SC.

Physics: C. A. CHANT, M.A., PH.D.

Physiology: A. B. MACALLUM, M.A., M.B., PH.D.

Embryology and Histology: W. H. PIERSOL, B.A., M.B.

Biology: B. A. BENSLEY, B.A., PH.D.

M. D. Examiners.

Medicine and Clinical Medicine: A. MCPHEDRAN, M.B.

Surgery and Clinical Surgery: I. H. CAMERON, M.B.

Clinical Gynæcology: J. A. TEMPLE, M.D., C.M.

Operative Obstetrics: A. H. WRIGHT, B.A., M.D.

Opthalmology and Otology: R. A. REEVE, B.A., M.D., LL.D.

Laryngology and Rhinology: G. R. MCDONAGH, M.D.

Applied Anatomy: A. PRIMROSE, M.B., C.M.

History of Medicine: A. B. MACALLUM, M.A., M.B., PH.D.

Electro Therapeutics and Life Assurance: N. A. POWELL, M.D., C.M.

Vaccination: C. SHEARD, M.D., C.M.

M. D., C. M., Examiners.

Anatomy, Descriptive and Practical: C. B. SHUTTLEWORTH, M.D., C.M.

Chemistry and Physics: W. T. STUART, M.D., C.M.

Materia Medica and Pharmacy: C. P. LUSK, M.D., C.M.

Physiology: C. SHEARD, M.D., C.M.

Medicine: H. C. PARSONS, B.A., M.D., C.M.

Surgery: F. LEM. GRASETT, M.D., C.M.

Pathology: H. B. ANDERSON, M.D., C.M.

Midwifery: C. A. TEMPLE, M.D., C.M.

LAW.

Law: A. R. CLUTE, B.A., LL.B.; A. W. BRIGGS, M.A., LL.B.

ENGINEERING.

Civil Engineering: W. T. JENNINGS, M. Inst., C.E.

Mechanical and Electrical Engineering: R. A. ROSS, E.E.

Mining Engineering: G. R. MICKLE, B.A.

APPLIED SCIENCE.

Mineralogy: T. L. WALKER, M.A., PH.D.

Geology: A. P. COLEMAN, M.A., PH.D.

Metallurgy and Assaying: G. R. MICKLE, B.A.

Thermodynamics and Hydraulics: R. W. ANGUS, B.A.Sc.; W. W. GRAY, B.A.Sc.

Theory of Construction: J. GALBRAITH, M.A., LL.D.

Properties of Materials: P. GILLESPIE, B.A.Sc.; C. H. C. WRIGHT, B.A.Sc.

Electricity and Magnetism: T. R. ROSEBRUGH, M.A.

Analytical and Applied Chemistry: J. W. BAIN, B.A.Sc.

Electro-Chemistry: W. L. MILLER, PH.D.

Geodesy and Astronomy: L. B. STEWART, D.T.S.

AGRICULTURE.

English: W. J. ALEXANDER, B.A., PH.D.

French and German: MISS A. ROWSOM, B.A.

Agricultural and Animal Chemistry: W. P. GAMBLE, B.S.A.

Botany: W. LOCHEAD, B.A., M.S.

Zoology and Entomology: F. SHERMAN, B.S.A.

Animal Husbandry: H. S. ARKELL, M.A., B.S.A.

Dairy Husbandry: H. H. DEAN, B.S.A.

Bacteriology: S. F. EDWARDS, B.S.A.

Physics: W. H. DAY, B.A.

Horticulture: H. L. HUTT, B.S.A.

Forestry: E. J. ZAVITZ, B.A., M.S.F.

Agriculture: J. BUCHANAN, B.S.A.

MUSIC.

Theory: A. HAM, Mus. Doc.

Practice: A. E. FAIRCLOUGH.

HOUSEHOLD SCIENCE.

Household Science: MISS A. L. LAIRD.

Physiology: A. B. MACALLUM, M.A., M.B., PH.D.; MISS C. C. BENSON, B.A., PH.D.

Hygiene: J. A. AMYOT, M.B.

Biology: A. G. HUNTSMAN, B.A.

PEDAGOGY.

Psychology applied to Pedagogy: F. TRACY, B.A., PH.D.

Ethics applied to Pedagogy: J. G. HUME, M.A., PH.D.

Science of Education, History and Criticism of Educational Systems: F. W. MERCHANT, M.A., D. Paed.

LOCAL EXAMINATIONS IN MUSIC.

Theory: A. HAM, Mus. Doc.; W. E. FAIRCLOUGH; C. L. M. HARRIS, Mus. Doc.

Organ: J. E. P. ALDOUS, B.A.; A. S. VOGT.

Singing: A. HAM, Mus. Doc.; R. S. PIGGOTT; D. ROSS; C. E. SAUNDERS, PH.D.; E. W. SCHUCH; R. TANDY.

Violin: F. E. BLACHFORD; R. POCOCKE.

Pianoforte: ST. JOHN HYTTENRAUCH; THOMAS MARTIN; H. PUDDICOMBE; J. D. A. TRIPP; A. S. VOGT; F. S. WELSMAN; W. O. FORSYTH; J. E. P. ALDOUS; H. M. FIELD; J. W. F. HARRISON.

PHYSICAL DRILL.

Theory: R. E. HOOPER.

Practice: A. WILLIAMS.

PHARMACY.

Pharmacy, Prescriptions and Dispensing: C. F. HEEBNER, PHM.B.

Chemistry: G. CHAMBERS, B.A., M.B.

Materia Medica: A. MOIR, PHM.B., M.B.

Botany: P. L. SCOTT, M.B.

DENTISTRY.

Presiding Examiner: J. B. WILLMOTT, D.D.S., M.D.S.

Physiology: F. A. CLARKSON, M.B.

Anatomy: F. N. G. STARR, M.B.

Jurisprudence: G. SILVERTHORN, M.B.

Chemistry: W. C. TROTTER, B.A., L.D.S., D.D.S.

Dental Materia Medica and Therapeutics: W. A. PIPER, L.D.S., D.D.S.

Prosthetic Dentistry: J. R. MITCHELL, L.D.S., D.D.S.

Medicine and Surgery: M. A. MORRISON, L.D.S., D.D.S.

Operative Dentistry and Pathology: H. E. EATON, L.D.S., D.D.S.

Orthodontia: G. A. ROBERTS, L.D.S., D.D.S.

Practical Dentistry: G. G. HUME, L.D.S., D.D.S.

THE HONORABLE W. MORTIMER CLARK, LL.D.
Lieutenant Governor of Ontario.—VISITOR.

Governing Bodies.

BOARD OF TRUSTEES. ·

JOHN HOSKIN, LL.D., K.C., *(Chairman.)*

THE PRESIDENT OF THE UNIVERSITY *(Vice Chairman.)*

THE CHANCELLOR OF THE UNIVERSITY.

THE VICE-CHANCELLOR OF THE UNIVERSITY.

THE PRINCIPAL OF UNIVERSITY COLLEGE.

BYRON EDMUND WALKER, D.C.L.

JOHN HERBERT MASON, ESQ.

CASIMIR STANISLAS GZOWSKI, ESQ.

THE HONORABLE GEORGE ALBERTUS COX.

F. A. MOURÉ......................*Bursar.*

SENATE, 1905-1906.

(1) Ex officio members.

THE HON. THE MINISTER OF EDUCATION.

HON. SIR WILLIAM RALPH MEREDITH, LL.D., *Chancellor.*

HON. CHARLES MOSS, LL.D., *Vice-Chancellor.*

JAMES LOUDON, M.A., LL.D., *President of the University.*

MAURICE HUTTON, M.A., LL.D., *Principal of University College.*

JOHN HOSKIN, LL.D., K.C., *Chairman of Board of Trustees.*

REV. NATHANIEL BURWASH, M.A., S.T.D., LL.D.,
President of Victoria College.

REV. THOMAS CLARK STREET MACKLEM, M.A., D.D., LL.D.,
Provost of Trinity College.

Rev. Daniel Cushing, c.s.b., *Superior of St. Michael's College.*

Rev. James Patterson Sheraton, m.a., d.d., ll.d.,
Principal of Wycliffe College.

Rev. William MacLaren, d.d., *Principal of Knox College.*

Robert Ramsay Wright, m.a., b.sc., ll.d., *Dean of the Faculty of Arts.*

Richard Andrews Reeve, b.a., m.d., ll.d.,
Dean of the Faculty of Medicine.

John Galbraith, m.a., c.e., ll.d.,
Dean of the Faculty of Applied Science and Engineering.

Hon. Edward Blake, m.a., ll.d., k.c., m.p., *Ex-Chancellor.*

Hon. Sir William Mulock, m.a., ll.d., k.c., m.p., *Ex-Vice-Chancellor.*

(2) Appointed members.

William Robert Lang, d.sc.,

James McGregor Young, m.a.,

Arthur Philemon Coleman, m.a., ph.d.,
Representatives of the Professors and Associate Professors .in Arts and Law.

Alexander McPhedran, m.b.,

Alexander Primrose, m.b., c.m.,
Representatives of the Professors and Associate Professors in Medicine.

Rev. Michael Vincent Kelly, b.a., c.s.b.,

John Joseph Cassidy, m.d.,
Representatives of St. Michael's College.

Hon. Samuel Hume Blake, b.a., k.c.,

Newman Wright Hoyles, b.a., k.c., ll.d.,
Representatives of Wycliffe College.

Rev. James Ballantyne, b.a.,

John Andrew Paterson, m.a., k.c.,
Representatives of Knox College.

Rev. John Burwash, m.a., d.sc., ll.d.,
Representative of Victoria College.

William Henry van der Smissen, m.a.,
Representative of University College.

The Right Rev. Arthur Sweatman, d.c.l.,
Representative of Trinity College.

Zebulon Aiton Lash, Esq., k.c.,
Representative of the Law Society of Upper Canada.

William Pirritte Dyer, m.a., d.d.,
Representative of Albert College, Belleville.

GEORGE CHRISTIE CREELMAN, B.S.A.,
  Representative of the Ontario Agricultural College Guelph.

JAMES BRANSTON WILLMOTT, D.D.S., M.D.S.,
  *Representative of the Royal College of Dental Surgeons of
  Ontario.*

WILLIAM HENRY ELLIS, M.A., M.B.,
  Representative of the Ontario School of Practical Science.

NEWTON WESLEY ROWELL, ESQ.
  Representative of the Toronto College of Music.

CARL FREDERICK HEEBNER, PHM.B.,
  Representative of the Ontario College of Pharmacy.

ANDREW SMITH, V.S., EDIN., F.R.C.V.S.,
  Representative of the Ontario Veterinary College.

RICHARD BARRINGTON NEVITT, B.A., M.D.,
  Representative of the Ontario Medical College for Women.

(3) Elected members.

ALFRED BAKER, M.A.,
ALFRED TENNYSON DELURY, M.A.,
WILLIAM DALE, M.A.,
ALLEN BRISTOL AYLESWORTH, M.A.,
JOHN CUNNINGHAM MCLENNAN, B.A., PH.D.,
JAMES CHISHOLM, B.A.,
WILLIAM JAMES LOUDON, B.A.,
ARCHIBALD BYRON MACALLUM, M.A., M.B., PH.D.,
JAMES HENRY COYNE, B.A.,
WILLIAM THOMAS WHITE, B.A.,
GEORGE MACKINNON WRONG, M.A.,
JOHN KING, M.A.,
  *Representatives of the Graduates in Arts of University
  College.*

REV. ALFRED HENRY REYNAR, M.A., LL.D.,
HON. JOHN JAMES MACLAREN, M.A., LL.D.,
ABRAHAM ROBERT BAIN, M.A., LL.D.
LEWIS EMERSON HORNING, B.A., PH.D.,
CHARLES CANNIFF JAMES, M.A.,
  *Representatives of the Graduates in Arts of Victoria
  College.*

REV. WILLIAM CLARK, F.R.S.C., M.A., D.C.L., D.D.
JAMES HENDERSON, M.A., D.C.L.,
JOHN AUSTIN WORRELL, M.A., D.C.L.,
ARCHIBALD HOPE YOUNG, M.A.,
  *Representatives of the Graduates in Arts of Trinity
  College.*

Hon. William Purvis Rochford Street, ll.b.,

William Renwick Riddell, b.a.; b.sc., ll.b.,

> *Representatives of the Graduates in Law.*

George Arthur Bingham, m.d.,

Irving Heward Cameron, m.b.,

Adam Henry Wright, b.a., m.d.,

James Algernon Temple, m.d.,

> *Representatives of the Graduates in Medicine.*

Charles Hamilton Mitchell, c.e.,

> *Representative of the Graduates in Applied Science and Engineering.*

Charles Alexander Mayberry, b.a., ll.b.,

James Elgin Wetherell, b.a.,

> *Representatives of the High School Teachers.*

The University Council.

THE PRESIDENT OF THE UNIVERSITY, *Chairman.*
PROFESSOR R. RAMSAY WRIGHT.
PROFESSOR BAKER.
PROFESSOR HUME.
PROFESSOR A. B. MACALLUM.
PROFESSOR FRASER.
PROFESSOR MAVOR.
PROFESSOR WRONG.
PROFESSOR PRIMROSE.
PROFESSOR CAMERON.
PROFESSOR McPHEDRAN.
PROFESSOR J. M. MacCALLUM.
PROFESSOR A. H. WRIGHT.
PROFESSOR REEVE.
PROFESSOR OLDRIGHT.
PROFESSOR KIRSCHMANN.
PROFESSOR LEFROY.
PROFESSOR LANG.
PROFESSOR MACKENZIE.
PROFESSOR YOUNG.
PROFESSOR COLEMAN.
PROFESSOR GALBRAITH.
PROFESSOR ELLIS.
PROFESSOR STEWART.
PROFESSOR C. H. C. WRIGHT.
PROFESSOR ROSEBRUGH.
ASSOCIATE PROFESSOR MILLER.
PROFESSOR WALKER.
PROFESSOR GRASETT.
PROFESSOR TEMPLE.
PROFESSOR POWELL.
PROFESSOR MICKLE.
THE PRINCIPAL OF UNIVERSITY COLLEGE.
THE PRESIDENT OF VICTORIA COLLEGE.
THE PROVOST OF TRINITY COLLEGE.
THE SUPERIOR OF ST. MICHAEL'S COLLEGE.
THE PRINCIPAL OF WYCLIFFE COLLEGE.
THE PRINCIPAL OF KNOX COLLEGE.
THE LIBRARIAN OF THE UNIVERSITY.

CONSTITUTION AND ADMINISTRATION OF THE UNIVERSITY.

The Constitution, powers and functions of the University are defined in ''The University Act, 1901.''

The management of the property, finances and academic business of the University is entrusted to the Board of Trustees, the Senate, Convocation, the University Council, and the Council of University College. The functions of these various bodies are exercised subject to supervision and control by the Crown, as hereafter explained.

1. THE CROWN.—The supreme authority is vested in the Crown. The Lieutenant Governor of Ontario is the Visitor of the University (as well as of University College) on behalf of the Crown, and his visitatorial powers may be exercised by commission under the great Seal. All annual appropriations made by the Board of Trustees are subject to the approval of the Lieutenant Governor in Council. All expenditures of endowment must be similarly authorised, and are subject also to ratification by the Legislative Assembly. The Crown exercises also a veto power as to certain statutes of the Senate and by-laws, rules and regulations of the Board of Trustees. Appointments in the University (as well as in University College) are made by the Crown, after such examination, inquiry and report as are considered necessary.

2. THE BOARD OF TRUSTEES.—The Board of Trustees consists of nine members, viz., the Chancellor, the Vice-Chancellor, the President of the University, the Principal of University College, and five persons appointed by the Lieutenant Governor in Council. The Board of Trustees is a body corporate with a common seal and power to hold lands for the purposes of the University and University College. All the property and effects of the University (as well as of University College) are vested in the Board of Trustees in trust. The Board has general powers with regard to the management, control and government of the property, endowments and income of the University and College, subject to the control of the Crown. In the discharge of its functions the Board makes

by-laws, rules and regulations regarding the investment of the funds, the selling and leasing of University properties, the letting of contracts, the appointment and removal of the Bursar and his assistants, clerks and other officers and servants of the University, the fixing of salaries, the fees to be paid by students, the annual appropriations and the transaction of other business.

3. THE SENATE.—The Senate consists of three classes of members: (1) *Ex officio* members; (2) Appointed members; and (3) Elected members. The *ex officio* members are the Minister of Education, the Chancellor, the President of the University, the Principal of University College, the Chairman of the Board of Trustees, the president or head of each federated university or college, the deans of the faculties of Arts, Law, Medicine, and Applied Science and Engineering, and all past Chancellors and Vice-Chancellors. The appointed members consist of three representatives appointed by the professors and associate professors in Arts and Law, two by the professors and associate professors in Medicine, two by every federated college, one by every federated university, one by University College, one by the Law Society of Upper Canada, and one by each affiliated institution (subject, however, in the latter case to certain restrictions). The elected members at present number thirty-one and represent the graduates in Arts who at graduation were enrolled in University College (twelve members), those in Victoria College and Trinity College (each five members), the graduates in Medicine (four members), in Law (two members), the graduates in Applied Science and Engineering (one member), and the High School teachers of the Province (two members)—the graduates in Medicine and Law of Victoria University voting along with the graduates of the University of Toronto in the same faculties.

The body thus composed is renewed, once in three years, when all except the *ex officio* members must retire, being eligible, however, for reappointment or re-election. The chairman of the Senate is the Chancellor, who is the elected representative of the whole body of graduates, or in his absence the Vice-Chancellor, who is elected by the Senate from among its members at its inaugural meeting after the triennal dissolution.

The functions of the Senate regard the general management of the academic work of the University, including the courses of study, the prescription of curricula in the various faculties and schools, the publication of the Calendars of the University and University College, the examinations for degrees, scholarships, prizes and certificates of honour, the granting of degrees, and the promotion of the interests and welfare of the University in cases not otherwise provided for by law. The Senate is empowered to make provision for the affiliation of any college, school or other institution established in the Province for the promotion of science or art, or for instruction in law, medicine, engineering, agriculture, or other useful branch of learning, and for the dissolution of such affiliation or the modification or alteration of the terms thereof.

It may also report to the Visitor on the general condition and progress of the University, and has power to inquire and report concerning the conduct, teaching and efficiency of members of the Faculties of the University of Toronto and of University College.

4. CONVOCATION.—Convocation consists of the whole body of graduates of the University, in all faculties. Except indirectly through its elected representatives, no part of the management of the University is exercised by it as a whole. It elects the Chancellor, and, in divisions according to faculty, it elects members of Senate as its representatives in Arts, Medicine, Law and Applied Science and Engineering. Any question relating to University affairs may be discussed by it, and a vote taken. The result of such discussion is communicated to the Senate, which must consider the representation made, and return to Convocation its conclusion thereon.

5. THE UNIVERSITY COUNCIL.—This body consists of the President, the senior Professor in each department of the University faculties of Arts, Medicine, Applied Science and Engineering, the Principal of University College, the Principal of each federated university or federated college and the Librarian of the University. The Council has power to deal with all matters affecting the discipline of students, to impose reasonable fines and to control all student societies or associations. It is also empowered under certain conditions to determine the time-tables, lectures and laboratory

3

work of the University, to grant dispensation from the lectures and laboratory work of the University and Colleges, and to authorise such lecturing or teaching in the University by others than the duly appointed professors and teachers as may be deemed expedient, and to prevent all lecturing or teaching not so authorised.

6. THE COUNCIL OF UNIVERSITY COLLEGE.—This body is composed of the Principal and the Professors and Associate Professors of the College. It has committed to it the direction and management of the College with full authority over and entire responsibility for the discipline (including the imposition of reasonable fines) of the undergraduates in relation to the lectures and other instruction of the professors, lecturers and other teachers of the College; and no lecturing or teaching of any kind may be carried on in the College by any other than the duly appointed professors or teachers without the authority of the Council.

7. FEDERATED INSTITUTIONS.—The following institutions are federated with the University, viz., Victoria College, Trinity College, Knox College, Wycliffe College and St. Michael's College. The President or other head of each is *ex officio* a member of the Senate and of the University Council. In addition, Knox, Wycliffe and St. Michael's Colleges each appoint two other representatives on the Senate. Victoria College and Trinity College each appoint one member, and the graduates of each elect five more representatives. All regular students matriculated in the University who are enrolled in University College or Victoria College or Trinity College and who enter their names with the Registrar of the University are entitled to free instruction in Arts in the University. But this provision does not include exemption from laboratory fees, nor does it apply to post-graduate instruction. When a federated college by arrangement with the University Council, teaches any part of the Arts course the Trustees may make a reduction in the fees of students taught in such College.

GENERAL INFORMATION FOR STUDENTS.

DISCIPLINE.

All students attending courses of instruction in the University of Toronto are responsible to the University Council for proper and orderly conduct within the University class rooms, buildings and grounds. The Council has authority to impose fines, and to use all other appropriate means of discipline.

THE LIBRARY.

The University Library occupies a separate building erected almost wholly by private benefaction, and completed in 1892. Besides a fire proof book room with a storage capacity of 100,000 volumes, it contains a reading room capable of seating upwards of 200 readers, a periodical room, seven departmental libraries, offices, cloak rooms and conversation rooms. The building is heated by steam throughout, thoroughly ventilated and supplied with electric light. The library contains at present upwards of 82,400 volumes together with upwards of 21,800 unbound pamphlets. It is provided, as far as the income permits, with the standard and current literature of all subjects taught in the University. In the departments of the natural and physical sciences it includes the principal journals and transactions of societies. In the departments of language and literature, the works of all authors of primary or secondary importance from the origins of each literature to the present time are available, as well as the principal philological and literary periodicals. Corresponding facilities are provided in the departments of philosophy, history and political science. The library is a circulating one for members of the Faculty, and a library of reference for students. The latter, however, are allowed under certain conditions the use of books at home outside of library hours, and students engaged in special work, requiring the consultation of books of reference, are allowed access to the stack room by the librarian on the recommendation of the professors. The departmental libraries are in charge of the professors in each department, and contain special refer-

ence collections of books. These rooms are intended for the instruction of advanced students, who may also at the discretion of their professors use the rooms and the books contained in them for private study. The conversation rooms, situated in the basement, are intended for the use of students who wish to withdraw for the purpose of discussion or combined study, to avoid disturbance of the reading room proper, where absolute quiet must be observed. Besides the general library, there are also special collections of periodicals and monographs situated in the Biological Building, the Medical Building, and in connection with the departments of Physics, Psychology and Law in the main University Building for the use of students and staff engaged in practical work.

THE PHYSICAL LABORATORY.

The Physical Laboratory, established in 1878, is situated in the western part of the Main Building, and consists of a set of rooms for elementary work, together with a number of special laboratories. The apparatus in the former is suitable for a general course of experiments in physics, including mechanics, geometrical and physical optics, heat, sound, electricity and magnetism. The special laboratories are equipped for the use of advanced undergraduate students taking the honour course in physics and for post-graduate students pursuing original investigations.

In connection with the laboratory is a well-equipped workshop in charge of a skilled mechanician who makes the necessary repairs and constructs most of the apparatus required for the work of research students.

THE PSYCHOLOGICAL LABORATORY.

The Psychological Laboratory, which was established in 1892, is situated in the west wing of the main University Building, in close proximity to the Physical Laboratory, the apparatus of which is available for some of the work in psychology. The Laboratory is well equipped for investigations in psycho-physics, psychological optics and acoustics and time relations of mental phenomena. There is in connection with the Laboratory, a small library containing the periodicals and the special literature of experimental psychology. On account of the increased number of undergraduates and graduates in the Philosophical Department and especially in order to facilitate the independent research of the graduates, it was found necessary in 1896 to extend the Psychological Laboratory by the addition of the rooms adjoining the Ethnological Museum and in 1900 by the addition of the rooms in the two upper storeys of the first house of the old Residence.

THE BIOLOGICAL BUILDING.

The Biological Building is formed of a central portion, which contains the Biological Museum, and east and west wings, the latter of which is chiefly occupied with the Anatomical Department. The east wing, on the other hand, contains the twelve rooms and laboratories of the Biological Department proper; on the ground floor is the large lecture room, accommodating upwards of 250 students, with suitable cloak rooms, etc., attached. In addition to this are private rooms, a preparation room, departmental library, and a large laboratory for the students of the Fourth Year. Above the lecture room on the first floor is situated the elementary laboratory used for the practical instruction of the large classes of students in the First Years in Arts and Medicine, while the remainder is occupied by a lecture room for small classes, a laboratory for students of the Third Year, a photographic room, a draughting room for the preparation of diagrams, a laboratory for vegetable physiology and bacteriology, and various private rooms. The second floor contains two rooms for the preparation and storage of museum specimens, two for the accommodation of live animals, and also two hot houses for use in connection with the practical courses in botany. In the basement are store rooms for alcoholic museum specimens and for glassware, a carpenter's shop and an aquarium.

The laboratories are provided with microscopes and all apparatus used by the students in morphological work; the advanced laboratories are furnished with necessary works of reference, and the lecture rooms with projection apparatus and very complete series of diagrams.

THE BIOLOGICAL MUSEUM.

The University Biological Museum forms the central portion of the Biological Building, and is open to the public. It is primarily intended as an educational museum for the stu-

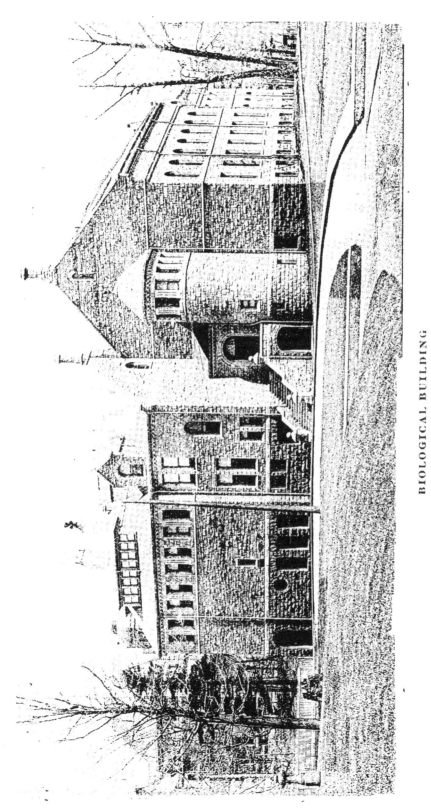

BIOLOGICAL BUILDING

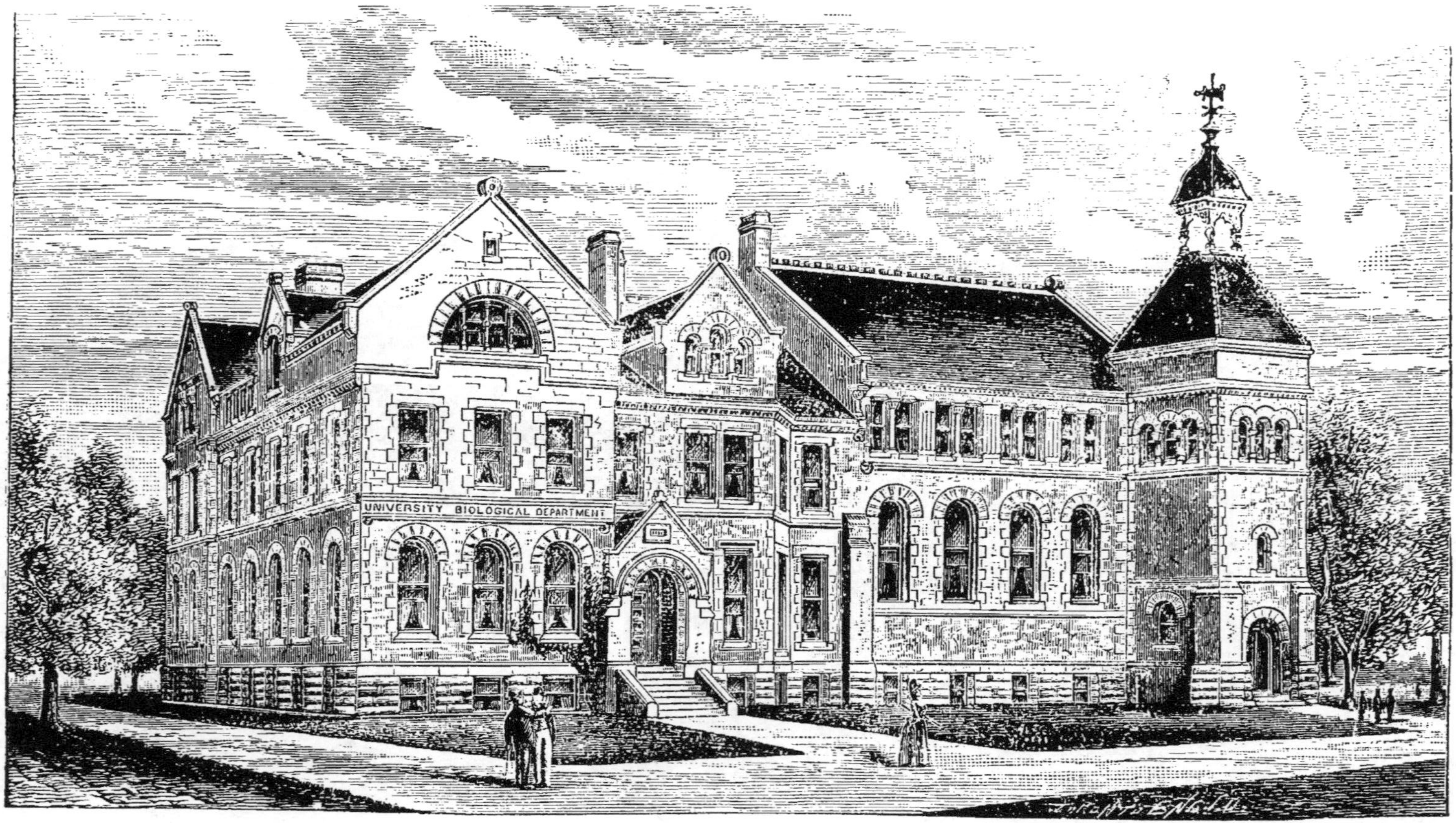

UNIVERSITY BIOLOGICAL DEPARTMENT.—(East Wing)

dents
has
arrang
as w
as p
the m

The
the w
gain

which
seven
hand
these
is arra

The
room,
vari
twe
dev
of in
smal
of d
mer
voted
tainin
fishes
ing sp
velop

A
guished
floor,
smal
gree
struc

Th
the
and
cases
spon
dat

dents taking biology as part of their University work, but it has proved also of great interest to the general public. It is arranged in such a way as to facilitate the most elementary as well as the most advanced studies, each specimen, as far as possible, being furnished with a printed label indicating the most salient points which it is designed to illustrate.

The public entrance to the Museum is approached from the west facade of the Biological Building, while the students gain access to the rooms through the eastern wing, in which the laboratories are situated. The interior of the Museum, which occupies two floors, is subdivided into four rooms, seventy-five by twenty-five feet in size, and amply lighted by handsome windows on the north and south sides. Three of these rooms are devoted to animal biology, while the fourth, is arranged for the illustration of vegetable biology.

The public entrance opens into the north ground floor room, the wall cases of which contain stuffed specimens of the various orders of mammals, while the free-standing cases between the windows illustrate the comparative anatomy and development of that class. All the show cases are constructed of iron and plate glass, those destined for the exhibition of smaller specimens standing on wooden storage cases, built of cherry and cedar, and containing skins and other specimens for private study. The south ground floor room is devoted to the remaining vertebrate classes, the wall cases containing stuffed specimens of birds, reptiles, batrachians and fishes, and the smaller cases between the windows containing specimens illustrating the comparative anatomy and development of these classes.

A handsome staircase decorated with busts of distinguished biologists connects the ground floor with the first floor; a number of wall cases in ascending series contains a small collection of fossils from all parts of the world, as a graphic illustration of the relative position of the fossiliferous strata, and of their characteristic remains.

The south first floor contains illustrative specimens of all the remaining branches of the animal kingdom, the arthropods and molluscs being exhibited in the wall cases and the table cases standing in the alcoves of these, while the protozoa, sponges, coelenterates, echinoderms and worms are accommodated in the cases between the windows.

Although the Natural History Museum suffered considerable losses on the occasion of the University fire, these fortunately did not involve the large collection of models and specimens most useful from the educational point of view, while the generosity of public bodies and private individuals has largely repaired the losses referred to, so that the Museum will be found to constitute a most important addition to the instruction furnished in the lecture rooms and laboratories.

THE PHYSIOLOGICAL LABORATORY.

The Physiological Laboratory occupies the southern section of the new Medical Building. It contains a series of laboratories, constructed on the "unit" system, six of which are devoted to experimental physiology and five to physiological chemistry. These rooms are equipped to furnish complete courses in these subjects to classes of as many as one hundred and fifty students at any one time. There are also laboratories for special courses in these subjects, and in addition a series of small research rooms, each for individual workers on some special topic in bio-chemistry or physiological histology.

THE CHEMICAL LABORATORY.

The Chemical Building was completed in 1895. It contains in addition to two lecture rooms with accommodation for 300 and 100 students, respectively, special laboratories for qualitative analysis, quantitative analysis, organic preparations, physical chemistry, gas analysis, combustion and furnace operations, and for the prosecution of original investigation. The total number of working places in these laboratories exceeds 200.

GEOLOGICAL AND MINERALOGICAL LABORATORIES.

By the erection of the new Chemistry and Mineralogy Building on College Street the University has secured for the first time really modern laboratory equipment for the departments of Geology and Mineralogy.

For students of science generally brief courses are given in laboratory work, especially in personal examination of type sets of rocks, fossils, minerals and crystal models. These laboratory exercises serve to illustrate the introductory didactic instruction.

For the encouragement of pure crystallography the laboratories are supplied with goniometers of the various types, crystal models, appliances for the cutting of oriented crystal sections and for the physical examination of the same. Practical Petrography is carried on in rooms provided with type sets of rocks, both macroscopic and microscopic. Advanced students are taught to make thin sections of rocks and fossils and to study them microscopically. Students in Palæontology are given instruction in the preparation of material for study and are afforded an opportunity of examining type series of specimens.

The laboratory for the preparation of thin sections of rocks, minerals and fossils is provided with electric diamond saws and grinding appliances for the various types of work incidental to the preparation of thin sections and museum material.

A room is also provided for advanced work in Cartography and Geological Surveying.

The departments possess 28 petrological microscopes and five of other types so that it is now possible to provide advanced students with instruments and sets of thin sections for their own especial use. The blowpipe laboratory contains 156 lockers, specially designed for apparatus for students. All students before being admitted to the laboratories are required to make a deposit to cover the cost of breakages during the session.

THE GEOLOGICAL AND MINERALOGICAL MUSEUM.

The large collections of the geological, palæontological and mineralogical departments are constantly being added to, and contain much valuable and interesting material, but are, at present, housed in temporary rooms. The fine Ferrier collection of minerals is in a small room at the west end of the new School of Science Building; the rich collections of fossils provided by Mr. B. E. Walker and Mr. Wm. Mackenzie are now being placed in cases which are to be arranged temporarily in the large lecture room at the east end of the same building; and the Bureau of Mines collection is still in boxes at the Parliament Buildings.

The Geological and Mineralogical Laboratories have been removed from their old quarters to the new building on College Street.

THE ETHNOLOGICAL MUSEUM.

The Ethnological Museum is situated in the second storey of the main University Building. It contains that part of the ethnological collection which was saved from the fire of 1890, together with the additions which have been made since that time. There is a fair collection of skulls, including ancient Egyptian and Roman skulls and models of the Neanderthal, Cro-Magnon, and other famous skulls. There are also interesting palæolithic implements from the English and French Drift, and the beginning of a good collection of stone implements from various parts of Canada.

UNIVERSITY PUBLICATIONS.

Under the general title of "University of Toronto Studies," a publication in the interests of scholarship. and research is issued, containing selected papers by members of the University. It is supported by a small grant from the provincial government. The committee of management represents the faculties of the University, University College Victoria College and the School of Practical Science. The President of the University is chairman of the committee, and the Librarian is general editor of the publications. From the nature of the publication, there is no regularity of issue, but as papers are accepted and recommended for publication, they are published to the extent of the funds available, without regard to any consideration except that of their value as contributions to the literature of learning.

For lists of studies published to January, 1906, see Appendix.

PUBLIC LECTURES.

In addition to the regular courses of instruction, a number of public lectures on special subjects of interest are delivered annually under the auspices of the University, on Saturday afternoons, by members of the faculty and others whose services are given voluntarily in this work. The lectures cover a large variety of topics, and those delivered hitherto have been numerously attended by the public, as well as by the students of the University. For the list of subjects and lecturers during 1905-1906, see Appendix.

STUDENT SOCIETIES.

Various societies and associations have been organised for the promotion of social intercourse, literary and scientific activity, music and athletics. For list of officers of these societies, see Appendix.

GYMNASIUM AND ATHLETIC GROUNDS.

The University Gymnasium was completed and equipped in 1893. In 1894, additions were made to the front of the building in which the Gymnasium is situated, consisting of committee rooms and a large hall for public meetings. This additional accommodation is available for the work of the various student societies and for academic purposes. Applications for the use of rooms, accompanied by a list of officers and a copy of the constitution of the society making application, must be made to the President at the beginning of the session, or from time to time as occasion requires. Arrangements have also been made by which recognised societies may obtain the use of committee rooms on application to the janitor of the building.

The Gymnasium is fully provided with the best and most modern appliances for physical culture, and contains a running track, shower baths and swimming bath, besides the necessary dressing rooms and other conveniences. A competent instructor in gymnastics is in constant attendance to superintend and direct the exercises of students. In addition to the lawn in front of the main University Building and the campus in the rear, a large plot of ground on Devonshire Place has been prepared and set apart as an Athletic Field. By this addition the facilities for football, cricket, tennis and other outdoor athletic sports are doubled, as compared with previous accommodation; and by these grounds, in conjunction with the Gymnasium, ample opportunity is afforded to all students for healthful exercise and physical development. To assist in meeting the expenses of the Gymnasium, a nominal annual fee is imposed on those who avail themselves of its advantages. The supervision of all athletic matters has been entrusted by the Council to the Athletic Association, consisting of members appointed from the faculty and representatives of the students. All applications of clubs for the use of grounds must be made annually to this board. All such applications must be accompained by a list of officers. In the case of new clubs, the list of officers must be accompanied by particulars as to the organisation and objects of the club making application.

A diploma in gymnastics and physical drill is granted to those who fulfil the requirements of the curriculum prescribed therefor by the Senate.

UNDERGRADUATE UNION.

Through the efforts of the faculty, graduates, undergraduates and friends of the University, this organisation was established during the session of 1900-1901. It has for its object the promotion of social intercourse among the students of the various faculties, colleges and schools. Apartments for the accommodation of the Union have been provided in a portion of the building formerly occupied by the College Residence.

DINING HALL.

In October, 1900, the Dining Hall, formerly belonging to the College Residence, was reopened. Under the management of a representative committee, students are provided with meals at moderate rates. Full particulars may be obtained at the Dining Hall Office in the Dean's House.

LODGING AND BOARD.

Lodging and board are readily obtainable in numerous private boarding houses within convenient distance of the University, at a cost of from three dollars upwards for comfortable lodging with board; or rooms may be rented at a cost of from one dollar per week upwards, and board obtained separately at moderate rates. A list of accredited boarding houses is kept by the Secretaries of the Young Men's Christian Associations of University College and Victoria College, and students are recommended to consult them with reference to the selection of suitable accommodation.

RESIDENCES.

For Men.

TRINITY COLLEGE...............REV. T. C. STREET MACKLEM, *Provost.*
ST. MICHAEL'S COLLEGE.............REV. FATHER CUSHING, *Superior.*
WYCLIFFE COLLEGE.................REV. T. R. O'MEARA, *Principal.*
KNOX COLLEGE................REV. WM. MACLAREN, D.D., *Principal.*

For Women.

QUEEN'S HALL.........................MRS. JOHN CAMPBELL, *Dean.*
ANNESLEY HALL.................MISS M. E. T. ADDISON, B.A., *Dean.*
ST. HILDA'S COLLEGE...............MISS M. CARTWRIGHT, *Principal.*

INFORMATION FOR STUDENTS IN MEDICINE.

The twentieth session since the re-establishment of the Medical Faculty of the University of Toronto will commence on Monday, the 1st of October, 1906, when the opening lecture will be delivered at 8.30 p.m.

DEGREES.

The degree of M.B. is given to the students who have matriculated and who have completed the prescribed course of study and passed the examinations required. The degree of M.D. is conferred on Bachelors of Medicine of at least one year's standing who have presented an approved thesis or who have passed a prescribed examination.

ENTRANCE.

Candidate for a degree must pass the Junior Matriculation examination, unless (1) they possess a degree in Arts, not being an honorary degree, from any Canadian or British University; or, (2) have already matriculated in the faculty of Arts or in the faculty of Law in this University; or, (3) have been registered as matriculates in the College of Physicians and Surgeons of Ontario. Candidates may delay Matriculation until any time before the Second examination for the degree of M.B., but if possible candidates should matriculate before commencing their medical studies.

INSTRUCTION.

The course of instruction given by the faculty of Medicine prepares students primarily for the degree of M.B., and for the license of the Ontario College of Physicians and Surgeons, but it fulfils the requirements of other Canadian and British Universities and it aims at giving the student such a training in the sciences as is now exacted of all those who desire to obtain any British medical qualification in addition to a Canadian one.

The new building of the faculty of Medicine has been completed, and is fully equipped. A detailed description of it will be found elsewhere in the calendar. With the completion of this building, a series of laboratories and lecture theatres is provided on the University grounds where the most ample facilities are afforded for both the practical and didactic instruction of students in every department embraced in the medical curriculum. The laboratories of the new building will be devoted solely to the departments of Physiology and Pathology, and in addition to the provision made for instruction of undergraduate students, a series of special laboratories is to be found, fully equipped for research work. As heretofore, lectures and demonstrations will be given in the Biological, Chemical, Physical and Anatomical Laboratories and lecture rooms of the University. It is impossible to provide more complete and efficient accommodation for the teaching of scientific medicine than that which exists in the University of Toronto to-day.

Clinical instruction is given in the Toronto General Hospital, the Mercer Eye and Ear Infirmary, the Burnside Lying-in Hospital, the Hospital for Sick Children, St. Michael's Hospital and other medical charities of Toronto. The facilities for clinical instruction have been very greatly improved, and the student has the fullest opportunities for making a thorough examination of all the cases of disease which are found in the wards and out-patient rooms of the hospitals. The students are arranged in small classes (of from twelve to fourteen) in order to facilitate this, and to enable the clinical teachers to give as much personal instruction as possible to each student.

The hospital facilities provided for the instruction of students in connection with the University will be greatly augmented in the immediate future. The Toronto General Hospital Trust will be reconstituted and a new and modern hospital will be built where an equipment for the scientific practice of medicine and surgery will be provided second to none on the continent in efficiency. Already upwards of a million dollars have been subscribed to further the building project. The munificent gift of $100,000 by Mr. Cawthra Mulock, will provide unsurpassed accommodation for the treatment of patients in the outdoor department, and will afford exceptional facilities for the instruction of students.

The faculty has in the General Hospital a laboratory for clinical pathology and chemistry, which has been furnished

4

with microscopes and all apparatus required for the examination of pathological fluids and specimens; and students, when they act as clinical clerks, will be admitted to all the privileges of the laboratory.

In the department of anatomy, the arrangements for instruction are now unsurpassed. In addition to other methods of illustrating anatomy, there will be courses in which the projection microscope will be employed to demonstrate to large classes the relational structure of the different parts of the body as exhibited in frozen sections. In materia medica also the course of instruction conforms to the most advanced methods.

The faculty has spared no expense in making the arrangements for medical instruction perfect, and is convinced that these, added to the unrivalled facilities offered by the University laboratories for the study of chemistry, physics, biology, anatomy, histology, physiology and pathology, will furnish the fullest opportunities to the student for acquiring a medical education of the most advanced and most progressive character.

Attention is directed to the recent establishment of a Museum of Hygiene.

EXAMINATIONS.

In addition to the Matriculation examination, candidates are required to pass four examinations, which must be taken in the following order: the First at the end of the first session; the Second at the end of the second session; the Third at the end of the third session, and the Final at the end of the fourth session.

NEW SCIENCE COURSE ADAPTED FOR STUDENTS IN MEDICINE.

The special attention of students entering Medicine is directed to the recent enactment of the University Senate instituting a new curriculum in science leading to the degree of Bachelor of Arts. This course, entitled the honour department of Biological and Physical Sciences, is specially adapted for students who intend entering eventually upon Medicine, and embraces the purely science subjects which are demanded of students in the primary years of Medicine. It will therefore be possible in the future for a candidate who has obtained his Arts degree in this course to enter immediately the Third Year of Medicine, and he will be qualified to present himself for the degree of Bachelor of Medicine two years after graduating in Arts. In other words, it is possible for one to obtain the degrees of Bachelor of Arts and Bachelor of Medicine after six years' study at the University.

The very great advantages of this course to a student entering Medicine are obvious. The preliminary science subjects of the course in Medicine are taught in much greater detail in the Arts course, as in the latter is included advanced laboratory and experimental work, such as is not required in the purely Medical course of studies. Further, the student is required to become proficient in modern languages, an acquirement which is of great value to the student of modern scientific Medicine.

This new course not only affords opportunity for wider culture and greater scientific attainment than is possible in the more limited four years' course in Medicine, but it fits one for a much wider field of usefulness after graduation. The graduate who has taken the science course in Arts and subsequently that of Medicine is qualified to devote his life to the purely scientific side of Medicine if he should so elect after leaving the University, and, moreover, he is undoubtedly better fitted to practice his profession should he desire to prepare himself for that alone.

Students may also combine the courses in Arts and Medicine to a less extent by proceeding to graduation in Arts through any one of the honour departments of biology, chemistry, geology and mineralogy and physics, certain courses and examinations in these departments being accepted as equivalent to similar courses and examinations in the faculty of Medicine.

MEDICAL COUNCIL REQUIREMENTS.

A student desirous of obtaining a license to practice medicine in Ontario must pass the July Matriculation examination of the University of Toronto, including the subjects physics and chemistry, which entitle him to be registered as a medical student. A fifth year of study is now demanded by the Ontario Medical Council. To meet this requirement a course of instruction has been arranged; students taking this course will have the opportunity of doing special work in the hospitals and laboratories, and they will be permitted to attend whatever didactic lectures they may desire.

For all information not covered by this announcement, the intending student should apply to the Registrar. or to Professor A. Primrose, The Medical Laboratories, University of Toronto.

THE MEDICAL BUILDING.

The completion of the Medical Building provides the necessary accommodation for the rapidly increasing classes.

This building, which cost $125,000, is situated between the University Library and the anatomical wing of the Biological Department. An additional $50,000 has been expended on equipment.

It is three storeys in height in front, with an additional storey and sub-basement in the wings, which extend eastward. Two large lecture rooms are provided which flank the main building; the larger has accommodation for about three hundred and fifty students; the smaller for about two hundred students.

In the south wing, in what may be called the basement storey, are situated caretaker's quarters, lavatories, recreation rooms and reading rooms for the students; in the same storey in the north wing is placed a large museum of hygiene.

The three main floors of the building are arranged upon what has been called the unit-system, a unit room being thirty feet long by twenty-three feet deep, lighted on its long face by two large windows.

These rooms may be united so as to form large laboratories or may be cut in two where it is necessary to have smaller rooms.

The south wing is occupied by the Arts department of Physiology, whilst the main portion of the building and the north wing accommodate the final departments of Medicine.

On the ground floor in the main portion are situated in front the Dean's room, a large faculty room, a laboratory and a library, behind is placed a large pathological museum.

In the north wing in this floor are placed a chart and preparation room behind the lecture theatre, preparation and store rooms for the pathological museum, and laboratories for gross pathology.

The second and third floors in the same wing and in front contain the laboratories of pathological histology and bacteriology with rooms for the Professor of Pathology and demonstrators, and unit rooms for small special classes.

In the north wing on the third floor units are occupied by the Provincial Board of Health for its bacteriological, and chemical laboratories.

An interesting feature of the building is the provision which is made for research students by the presence of a series of small rooms in front of the south lecture room, each large enough to accommodate one or two workers.

The ventilation is of the most modern type, and each room provided with both gas and electric light.

The building in every way is thoroughly up-to-date, and in the extent of window light for the laboratories is probably unique on this continent

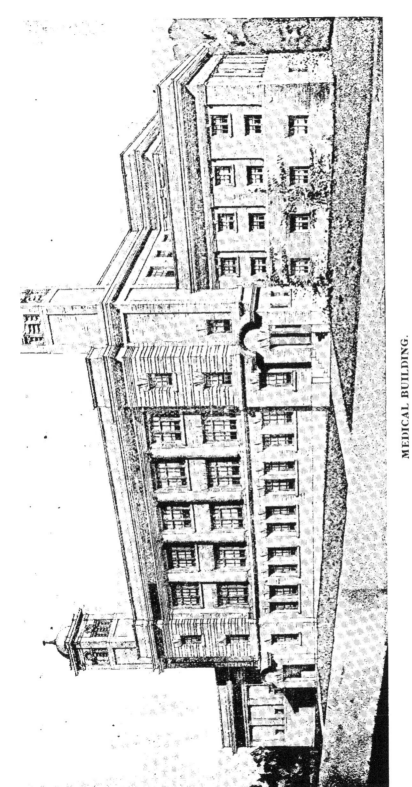

MEDICAL BUILDING.

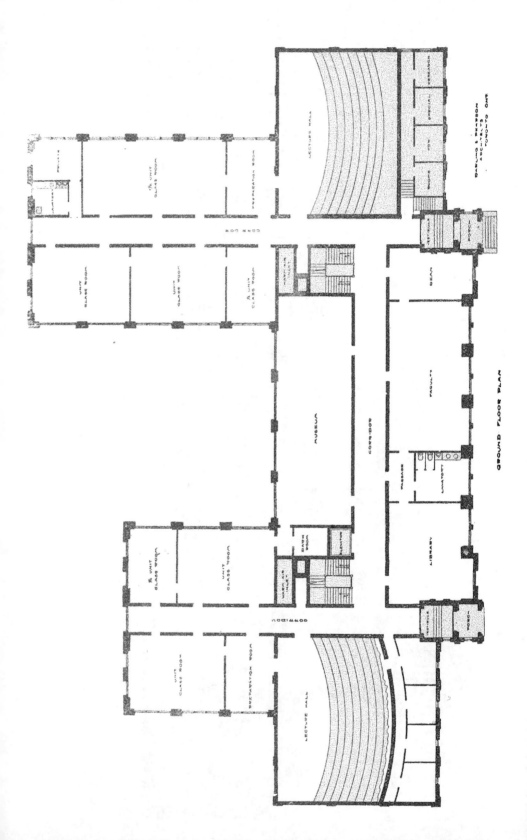

GROUND FLOOR PLAN

DARLING & PEARSON
ARCHITECTS
TORONTO ONT

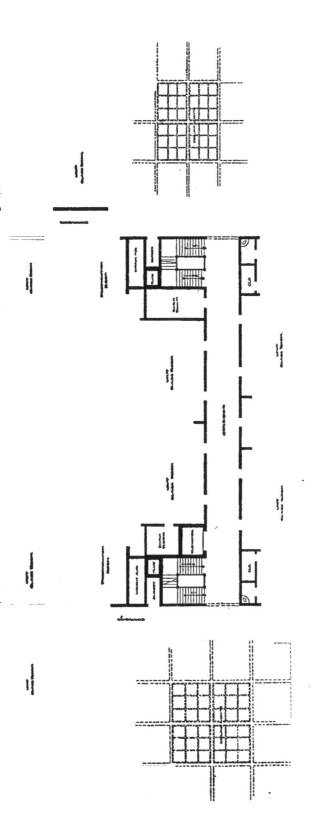

—FIRST FLOOR PLAN—

MEDICAL BUILDING.

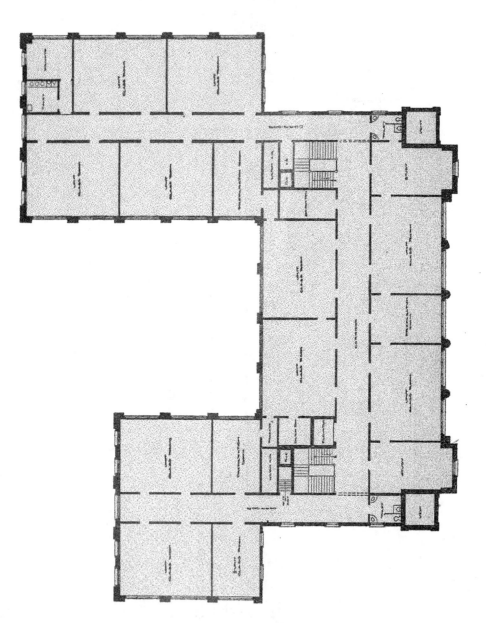

—SECOND FLOOR—

The Faculty.

President of the University..............JAMES LOUDON, M.A., LL.D.

Dean of the Faculty..................R. REEVE, B.A., M.D., LL.D.

Secretary........................A. PRIMROSE, M.B., C.M., Edin.

Professores Emeriti.

M. H. AIKINS, B.A., M.D.   J. H. RICHARDSON, M.D.
W. W. OGDEN, M.D.   UZZIEL OGDEN, M.D.

Professors, Lecturers and Demonstrators.

ANATOMY.

Professor and Director of the Anatomical Department:
A. PRIMROSE, M.B., C.M., Edin.

Associate Professor: M. WILBERFORCE AIKINS, B.A., M.B., Tor.

Demonstrator: C. B. SHUTTLEWORTH, M.D., C.M., Trin., F.R.C.S., Eng.

Assistant-Demonstrators:

W. J. McCOLLUM, M.B., Tor.
W. J. O. MALLOCH, B.A., M.B., Tor.
S. W. WESTMAN, M.B., Tor.
GEORGE ELLIOTT, M.D., C.M., Trin.
E. R. HOOPER, B.A., M.B., Tor.
A. C. HENDRICK, M.A., M.B., Tor.
A. J. McKENZIE, B.A., LL.B., M.B., Tor.
D. McGILLIVRAY, M.B., Tor.
E. S. RYERSON, M.D., C.M., Trin.
F. W. MARLOW, M.D., C.M., Trin., F.R.C.S., Eng.
W. A. SCOTT, B.A., M.B., Tor., F.R.C.S., Eng.
C. J. COPP, M.D., C.M., Trin.
G. E. SMITH, B.A., M.B., Tor.

SURGERY.

Professors of Surgery and Clinical Surgery:
I. H. CAMERON, M.B., Tor., F.R.C.S. Eng., LL.D., Edin.
F. LeM. GRASETT, M.B., C.M., F.R.C.S., Edin.
G. A. PETERS, M.B., Tor., F.R.C.S., Eng.
L. TESKEY, M.D., C.M., Trin.

Associate-Professor of Clinical Surgery and Clinical Anatomy:
G. A. BINGHAM, M.D., C.M., Trin., M.B., Tor.

Associate-Professors of Clinical Surgery:
>A. PRIMROSE, M.B., C.M., Edin.
>
>N. A. POWELL, M.D., C.M., Trin., M.D., Bellevue, N.Y.
>
>W. OLDRIGHT, M.A., M.D., Tor.
>
>H. A. BRUCE, M.B., Tor., F.R.S.C., Eng.
>
>F. N. G. STARR, M.B., Tor.

Associate-Professor of Clinical Surgery, in charge of Orthopœdics:
>C. L. STARR, M.B., Tor.

Demonstrators of Clinical Surgery:
>W. MACKEOWN, B.A., M.B., Tor.
>
>C. A. TEMPLE, M.D., C.M., Trin.
>
>A. H. GARRATT, M.D., C.M., Trin.
>
>C. B. SHUTTLEWORTH, M.D., C.M., Trin., F.R.C.S., Eng.
>
>T. B. RICHARDSON, M.D., C.M., Trin., F.R.C.S., Edin.
>
>J. F. UREN, M.D., C.M., Trin.

PATHOLOGY.

Professor of Pathology and Bacteriology and Curator of the Museum and Laboratories: J. J. MACKENZIE, B.A., M.B., Tor.

Associate-Professor of Pathology and Bacteriology: J. A. AMYOT, M.B., Tor.

Laboratory-Assistant in Bacteriology:
>T. D. ARCHIBALD, B.A., M.B., Tor.

Demonstrators: G. SILVERTHORN, M.B., Tor.; C. J. WAGNER, M.B., Tor.

Assistant Demonstrators:
>W. H. PEPLER, M.D., C.M., Trin.
>
>H. C. PARSONS, B.A., M.D., C.M., Trin., M.R.C.P., Lond.
>
>M. M. CRAWFORD, M.B., Tor.
>
>F. A. CLARKSON, M.B., Tor.
>
>E. S. RYERSON, M.D., C.M., Trin.
>
>G. W. HOWLAND, B.A., M.B., Tor., M.R.C.P., Lond.

Assistant in Clinical Laboratory:
>M. H. V. CAMERON, M.B., Tor.

MEDICINE.

Professor of Medicine and Clinical Medicine: A. McPHEDRAN, M.B., Tor.

Associate-Professors of Medicine:
>R. D. RUDOLF, M.D., C.M., Edin., M.R.C.P., Lond.
>
>J. T. FOTHERINGHAM, B.A., Tor., M.D., C.M., Trin.

Professor of Clinical Medicine:
>J. L. DAVISON, B.A., Tor., M.D., C.M., Trin.

Associate-Professors of Clinical Medicine:

A. M. Baines, M.D., C.M., Trin.

W. P. Caven, M.B., Tor.

W. B. Thistle, M.B., Tor.

J. T. Fotheringham, B.A., Tor., M.D., C.M., Trin.

A. R. Gordon, M.B., Tor.

R. J. Dwyer, M.B., Tor. M.R.C.P., Lond.

H. B. Anderson, M.D., C.M., Trin.

Associates in Clinical Medicine:

G. Boyd, B.A., M.B., Tor.

R. D. Rudolf, M.D., C.M., Edin., M.R.C.P., Lond.

G. Chambers, B.A., M.B., Tor.

F. Fenton, M.D., C.M., Trin.

II. C. Parsons, B.A., M.D., C.M., Trin., M.R.C.P., Lond.

W. Goldie, M.B., Tor.

Tutors in Medicine: G. W. Howland, B.A., M.B., Tor., M.R.C.P., Lond.

D. McGillivray, M.B., Tor.

T. D. Archibald, B.A., M.B., Tor.

PREVENTIVE MEDICINE.

Professor of Preventive Medicine, Didactic and Clinical:

C. Sheard, M.D., C.M., Trin.

MATERIA MEDICA AND THERAPEUTICS.

Professor of Materia Medica, Pharmacology and Therapeutics:

J. M. MacCallum, B.A., M.B., Tor.

Demonstrator of Pharmacology: V. E. Henderson, M.A., M.B., Tor.

Demonstrator of Pharmacy: C. P. Lusk, M.D., C.M., Trin.

OBSTETRICS AND GYNÆCOLOGY.

Professor of Gynæcology and Operative Obstetrics:

J. Algernon Temple, M.D., C.M., McGill, LL.D., Tor.

Professor of Obstetrics: A. H. Wright, B.A., M.B., Tor.

Professor of Gynæcology: J. F. W. Ross, M.B., Tor.

Associate-Professor of Obstetrics and Pediatrics:

H. T. Machell, M.B., Tor.

Associate-Professor of Pediatrics: A. M. Baines, M.D., C.M., Trin.

Associates in Obstetrics: K. C. McIlwraith, M.B., Tor., F. Fenton, M.D., C.M., Trin.

OPHTHALMOLOGY AND OTOLOGY.

Professors: R. A. REEVE, B.A., M.B., LL.D., Tor.
G. S. RYERSON, M.D., C.M., Trin.
G. H. BURNHAM, M.D., Tor., F.R.S.C., Edin.
Associate-Professor: C. TROW, M.D., C.M., Trin.
Associate: J. M. MacCALLUM, B.A., M.B., Tor.

LARYNGOLOGY AND RHINOLOGY.

Professor: G. R. McDONAGH, M.D., Tor.
Associate-Professor:
D. J. GIBB WISHART, B.A., Tor., M.D., C.M., McGill.
Associate: G. BOYD, B.A., M.B., Tor.

HYGIENE.

Professor: W. OLDRIGHT, M.A., M.B., Tor.

PHYSIOLOGY AND PHYSIOLOGICAL CHEMISTRY.

Professor: A. B. MACALLUM, M.A., M.B., Tor., Ph.D., Johns Hopkins, F.R.S.
Demonstrator: V. E. HENDERSON, M.A., M.B., Tor.
Assistant Demonstrators:
A. C. HENDRICK, M.A., M.B., Tor.
A. HENDERSON, B.A., Tor.,
MISS M. L. MENTEN, B.A., Tor.
E. M. HENDERSON, B.A., Tor.
W. F. McPHEDRAN, B.A., Tor.
W. H. CRONYN, B.A., M.B., Tor.
J. GRAHAM, M.B., Tor.
E. FIDLER, B.A., Tor.
J. S. GRAHAM, M.B., Tor.
G. C. GRAY.
W. B. LARGE, B.A.
J. MacLACHLAN.
F. R. MILLER, B.A , Tor.

TOXICOLOGY.

Professor: W. H. ELLIS, M.A., M.B., Tor.

MEDICAL JURISPRUDENCE.

Professor: N. A. POWELL, M.D., C.M., Trin., M.D., Bellevue, N.Y.

MENTAL DISEASES.

Extra-Mural Professors: N. H. BEEMER, M.B., Tor.

C. K. CLARKE, M.B., Tor.

BIOLOGY.

Professor of Biology:

R. RAMSAY WRIGHT, M.A., B.Sc., Edin., LL.D., Tor.

Lecturer in Elementary Biology and Histology:

W. H. PIERSOL, B.A., M.B., Tor.

Class Assistant in Biology and Histology: M. D. MCKICHAN, B.A.,

M.B., Tor.

A. J. MCKENZIE, B.A., LL.B. M.B., Tor.

E. A. MCCULLOCH, B.A., M.B., Tor.

W. A. SCOTT, B.A., M.B., Tor., F.R.C.S., Eng.

E. C. COLE, B.A., Tor.

C. M. HINCKS, B.A., Tor.

H. G. WILSON, B.A., Tor.

CHEMISTRY.

Professor: W. R. LANG, D.Sc., Glasg.

Associate Professor of Medical Chemistry:

W. T. STUART, M.D., C.M., Trin.

Lecturers: F. B. ALLAN, M.A., PH.D.; F. B. KENRICK, M.A., PH.D.

Assistants: E. L. C. FORESTER, M.A.; R. L. CLARK, B.A.;

R. B. Stewart, B.A; J. A. M. DAWSON, B.A.

Private Assistant: W. P. KAUFMANN.

Fellow; R. E. DeLURY, M.A.

PHYSICS.

Professor: JAMES LOUDON, M.A., LL.D., Tor.

Associate Professor and Director of the Physical Laboratory:

J. C. MCLENNAN, B.A., PH.D.

Lecturer: C. A. CHANT, B.A., Tor., PH.D., Harv.

Assistant Demonstrator:

H. F. DAWES, M.A., Tor.

MISS L. B. JOHNSON, M.A., Tor.

F. D. MEADER, B.A., Tor.

Class Assistants: C. A. FRENCH,

A. E. JOHNS,

J. K. ROBERTSON,

C. WOODHOUSE,

MISS F. M. ASHALL,

MISS E. J. WILLIAMS,

6

Remsen's Organic Chemistry. Perkin & Kip-
Chemistry. Books of Reference: Bernthsen's.
ustry (English edition). Richter's Organic
2 ols.) (English Edition).

ory work of the First year now commences
t ve and qualitative experiments illustrating the
principles of Chemistry, this is followed by work
e related to analytical chemistry to which the
f le session is devoted.

ary work of the Second year includes elemen-
r: analysis, with special application to clinical
I anitary science, and the analysis of urine;
analysis as applied in toxicology and medi-

rking in the laboratory are provided with the
pratus on making a deposit of three dollars* at
t ent of the session, which will be returned at
te the following charges have been deducted

e t of all apparatus broken or destroyed.

fies for breach of laboratory rules.

icae will be given for the practical work unless
he passed the practical examinations conducted
es on.

adition to the fee of three dollars mentioned as "Chem-
v upply Fee," on page 133.

COURSES OF LECTURES.

Methods of Instruction, Winter Session, 1906-1907.

CHEMISTRY.

Professor: W. R. LANG.

Associate Professor of Medical Chemistry: W. T. STUART.

Lecturers: F. B. ALLAN, M.A., PH.D.; F. B. KENWICK, M.A., PH.D.

Assistants: E. L. C. FORSTER, R. L. CLARK, B.A., R. B. STEWART, B.A., J. A. M. DAWSON, B.A.

Fellow: R. E. DELURY.

All lectures and practical work will be given in the Chemical Building. The students of the First year attend a course of lectures delivered twice a week in the large lecture theatre, on Inorganic Chemistry. This course embraces the study of the non-metallic and metallic elements and of their principal compounds, based on Mendelejeff's classification of the elements.

Tutorial Classes: In addition to the Lectures the class is divided into sections, each of which meets one day a week for further instruction in Arithmetical Chemistry.

Text-Books: Remsen's College Chemistry. Newth, Inorganic Chemistry. Newell, Descriptive Chemistry. Bailey's Tutorial Chemistry (2 vols.). Book of Reference—Bloxam.

The instruction given in practical chemistry includes a systematic course of laboratory work on qualitative analysis of inorganic salts, acids and bases.

The students of the Second year attend a course of lectures on Organic Chemistry, delivered twice a week. The principles of organic analyses and the basis on which the compounds of carbon are classified are explained, and the typical compounds and derivations of the "fatty" series specially described. An elementary study of the "aromatic" series is also included in the course.

*This is in addition to the fee of three dollars mentioned as "Chemical Laboratory Supply Fee," on page 122.

Textbooks: Remsen's Organic Chemistry. Perkin & Kipping's Organic Chemistry. Books of Reference: Bernthsen's. Organic Chemistry (English edition). Richter's Organic Chemistry (2 vols.) (English Edition).

The laboratory work of the First year now commences with quantitative and qualitative experiments illustrating the fundamental principles of Chemistry, this is followed by work more intimately related to analytical chemistry to which the latter part of the session is devoted.

The laboratory work of the Second year includes elementary volumetric analysis, with special application to clinical medicine and sanitary science, and the analysis of urine; and qualitative analysis as applied in toxicology and medicine.

Students working in the laboratory are provided with the necessary apparatus on making a deposit of three dollars* at the commencement of the session, which will be returned at its close after the following charges have been deducted from it:—

(1) The cost of all apparatus broken or destroyed.

(2) Any fines for breach of laboratory rules.

No certificate will be given for the practical work unless the student has passed the practical examinations conducted during the session.

*This is in addition to the fee of three dollars mentioned as "Chemical Laboratory Supply Fee," on page 133.

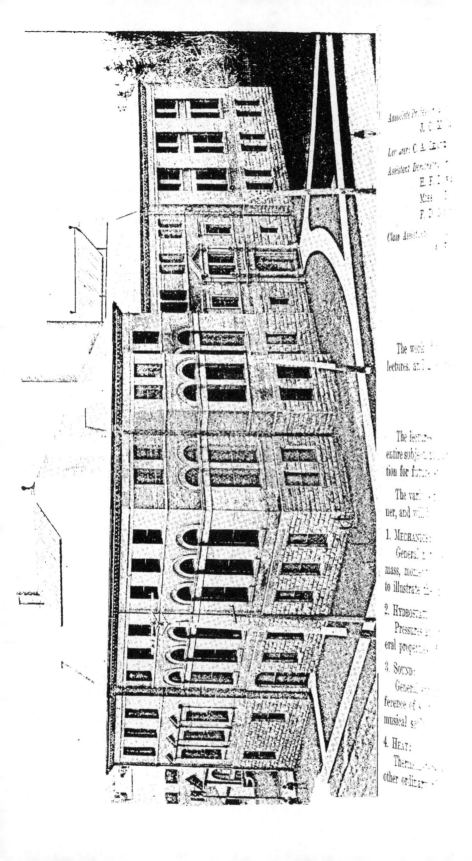

Associate Pr...
J. ...

Lecturer: C. ...

Assistant De...
H. ...
Miss ...
F. ...

Class Assistant...

The work ...

lectures, and ...

The lectures ...

entire subject ...

tion for fut...

The var...

ner, and w...

1. MECHANICS:

General ...

mass, mo...

to illustrate ...

2. HYDROSTAT...

Pressures ...

eral propert...

3. SOUND:

General...

ference of ...

musical s...

4. HEAT:

Therm...

other ordinar...

PHYSICS.

Professor: J. Loudon.

Associate Professor and Director of the Physical Laboratory:
J. C. McLennan.

Lecturer: C. A. Chant.

Assistant Demonstrators:
H. F. Dawes.
Miss L. B. Johnson.
F. D. Meader.

Class Assistants: C. A. French,
A. E. Johns,
J. K. Robertson,
C. Woodhouse,
Miss F. M. Ashall.
Miss E. J. Williams,

The work of instruction in Physics consists of a series of lectures, and a course of practical work in the laboratories.

Lectures.

The lectures on Physics will give a concise outline of the entire subject, and are intended to form a satisfactory foundation for future study in other branches of science.

The various parts will be treated in an experimental manner, and will be considered in the following order:—

1. Mechanics:
General notions and terms, such as velocity, acceleration, mass, momentum, force, energy; together with calculations to illustrate the laws.

2. Hydrostatics:
Pressures and their transmission, specific gravity, and general properties of liquids and gases.

3. Sound:
General explanation of wave-motion, reflection and interference of sound, tuning forks, organ-pipes, strings, and the musical scale.

4. Heat:
Thermometers, expansion, specific heat, latent strings, and other ordinary phenomena.

5. LIGHT:

Laws of reflection and refraction, mirrors, prisms, lenses microscope and telescope, colour, double-refraction and polarization.

6. ELECTRICITY AND MAGNETISM:

Laws of magnetism; voltaic cell, chemical, magnetic and heating effect of the electric current; induction, the induction-coil, dynamo, etc.

The lectures will be given in Room 16, Main Building (West Wing).

Practical Work.

The Practical Work, consisting of a laboratory course of fifty hours, designed to illustrate the principles dealt with in the lectures, will be conducted by a number of Demonstrators under the supervision of the Director of the Laboratory.

Regulations.

Deposit Fee: Each student taking the laboratory course is required to make a deposit of two dollars ($2.00) before commencing work. All supplies, apparatus broken or destroyed and all fines will be charged against this deposit, which must be renewed when exhausted. At the close of the session cash balances will be returned on a day appointed for the purpose.

BIOLOGY.

Professor of Biology: R. RAMSAY WRIGHT.

Lecturer in Elementary Biology and Histology: W. H. PIERSOL.

Class Assistants in Biology and Histology: M. D. McKICHAN, B.A., M.B.; A. J. MACKENZIE, B.A., LL.B., M.B.; E. A. Mc-CULLOUGH, B.A., M.B.; W. A. SCOTT, B.A., M.B., F.R.C.S.; E. C. COLE, B.A.; C. M. HINCKS, B.A.; H. G. WILSON, B.A.

1. Students of the First year will attend a course of lectures on general biology, to be given twice a week throughout the session. This course of lectures is designed as an introduction of the whole range of biological studies. After a sketch of the scope and objects of these, the lectures will treat (1) of the fundamental principles of biology, as illustrated by the simplest animals and plants, (2) of typical forms of

higher plants in ascending order, (3) of typical forms of animals in a similar order, and (4) special reference will be made to those aspects of Biology of interest to students of Medicine.

2. A practical course of fifty hours' duration is conducted by Dr. Piersol in which various types are studied and which serves as an introduction to the use of the microscope.

3. A supplementary course of twenty-five lectures is given in connection with the foregoing.

4. A course of twenty-five lectures on embryology by the Professor will be chiefly devoted to the development of the external form of the organs and of the tissues of the human body, but the necessary comparative data for the proper understanding of these will be supplied by reference to the embryology of the amphibia and the birds. The student may consult the large collection of models of embryology in the Museum, which are now furnished with explanatory labels designed to supplement the instruction given in the lectures.

5. A similar series of twenty-five lectures on histology is designed to cover the general principles of Human Histology.

6. In illustration of the foregoing courses the Lecturer, with the aid of the assistants, will conduct a practical course on Histology and Embryology of one hundred hours. The student will have the opportunity of providing himself with a set of typical specimens illustrative of histology, and of studying a carefully selected series of embryological preparations, and of becoming acquainted with the methods employed in Histology and Embryology.

THE BIOLOGICAL MUSEUM.

The University Biological Museum forms the central portion of the Biological Buildings. It is primarily intended as an educational Museum for the students taking biology as part of their University work. It is arranged in such a way as to facilitate the most elementary as well as the most advanced studies, each specimen, as far as possible, being furnished with a printed label indicating the most salient points which it is designed to illustrate. The Museum, however, being open every afternoon, is also of great interest to the general public and attracts even greater numbers of visitors than the old Natural History Museum in the University Building.

The public entrance to the Museum is situated in the west façade of the Biological Buildings, while the students gain access to the rooms through the eastern wing, in which the laboratories are located. The interior of the Museum, which occupies two floors, is sub-divided into four rooms, seventy-five by twenty-five feet in size, amply lighted by handsome windows on the north and south sides. Three of these rooms are devoted to Animal Biology, while the fourth is being arranged for the illustration of Vegetable Biology.

The public entrance opens into the north ground-floor room, the wall-cases in which contain stuffed specimens of the various orders of Mammals, which the free-standing cases between the windows illustrate the comparative anatomy and development of that class. All the show-cases are constructed of iron and plate-glass, those destined for the exhibition of smaller specimens standing on wooden storage-cases, built of cherry and cedar, and containing skins and other specimens for private study. The south ground-floor room is devoted to the remaining vertebrate classes, the wall-cases containing stuffed specimens of birds, reptiles, batrachians and fishes, and the smaller cases between the windows containing specimens illustrating the comparative anatomy and development of these classes.

A handsome staircase decorated with busts of distinguished biologists connects the ground-floor and the first floor; a number of wall-cases in ascending series contains a small collection of fossils from all parts of the world, as a graphic illustration of the relative position of the fossiliferous strata, and of their characteristic remains.

The south first floor contains illustrative specimens of all the remaining branches of the animal kingdom, the arthropods and molluscs being exhibited in the wall-cases and the table cases standing in the alcoves of these, while the protozoa, sponges, coelenterates, echinoderms or worms are accommodated in the cases between the windows.

Although the Natural History Museum suffered considerable losses on the occasion of the University fire, these fortunately did not involve the large collection of models and specimens most useful from the educational point of view, while the generosity of public bodies and private individuals has largely repaired the losses referred to, so that the Museum will be found to constitute a most important addition to the instruction furnished in the lecture rooms and laboratories.

PHYSIOLOGY.

Professor of Physiology and Physiological Chemistry: A. B. MACALLUM.

Demonstrator: V. E. HENDERSON.

Assistant Demonstrators: A. C. HENDRICK, A. HENDERSON, E. M. HENDERSON, W. F. McPHEDRAN, W. H. CRONYN, J. GRAHAM, E. FIDLER, J. S. GRAHAM, J. MacLACHLAN, W. B. LARGE, F. R. MILLER, G. C. GRAY, MISS M. L. MENTEN.

Three courses of instruction are given in Physiology and Physiological Chemistry, one of which is primary, the others advanced.

1. The primary course, comprehending thirty lectures, with demonstrations, is given in the Easter Term and for students of the First year.

2. A laboratory course, equivalent to two hours a week throughout the session, will be required of each student of the First year. This course covering four months is devoted to Experimental Physiology. For this purpose the class is divided into groups of two, each couple of students working together on the whole course of experiments and throughout the period allotted for the same. Each group will be given the complete set of instruments necessary to carry out all the experiments required in the course, and will be expected to preserve for inspection all the graphic records which they may obtain. Each student will be expected to be thoroughly familiar with the proper use of all the apparatus given him.

3. The advanced course of lectures, which are four a week throughout the session, is arranged for the students of the Second year. It will comprehend the subjects, Physiology and Physiological Chemistry, and it will be specially adapted to the course of laboratory work which also each student is required to take. The course of lectures will begin with a discussion of the characters and classification of the more important chemical compounds of physiological origin, but subsequently, the chemistry of the tissues, and of the various

physiological fluids and excretions will be fully discussed in their natural order in the lectures on the functions of the organs.

4. An advanced laboratory course of six hours a week throughout the session is required of each student who takes the advanced course of lectures on Physiology and Physiological Chemistry.

This course is devoted to the physiology of nutrition, respiration, hearing, vision, and of the nervous system, to the practical examination of the chemistry of physiological compounds, of blood, lymph, muscle, the digestive fluids, bile, and urine, and the student will be expected to acquire a practical knowledge of the methods of Volumetric Analysis employed in the estimation of chlorides, and phosphates, and nitrogen in physiological fluids, and in the estimation of sugar, urea, and uric acid. The course in Hæmatology will comprehend the various methods of estimating the number of corpuscles of different kinds and of determining the amount of Hæmoglobin. For all these purposes the laboratories for Physiological Chemistry are specially arranged.

From time to time test examinations will be held to determine the student's practical knowledge and the results of these as well as of his general work in the laboratory will be used to determine his position in the University class lists.

In the primary and advanced courses the student will be required to make good all loss through breakage or otherwise.

ANATOMY.

Professor and Director of the Anatomical Department: A. PRIMROSE.

Associate-Professor: H. W. AIKINS.

Demonstrator: C. B. SHUTTLEWORTH.

Assistant Demonstrators: W. J. McCOLLUM, W. J. O. MALLOCH, S. W. WESTMAN, GEO. ELLIOTT, E. R. HOOPER, A. C. HENDRICK, A. J. McKENZIE, D. McGILLIVRAY, E. S. RYERSON, F. W. MARLOW, W. A. SCOTT, C. J. COPP, G. E. SMITH.

Lectures.—A course of lectures will be given in the Biological Department for students of the First and Second years; in this course the structure of the human body will be described in a systematic manner; the various organs of the body will be examined with their more important relations and connections. In order that the course may be more comprehensive certain principles in general morphology and development will be elucidated. The lectures will be illustrated by recent dissections, by wet and dry preparations and by drawings and diagrams. In the class-room a projection apparatus will be employed for the purpose of throwing upon a screen an enlarged view of the photographs, taken from the valuable preparations which are displayed for study in the Museum. This greatly facilitates the demonstration of anatomical structure before a large class; plates of these preparations will be distributed among the students.

Tutorial instruction will be given to limited classes for the purpose of studying osteology, and for the demonstration of the structure of the central nervous system and the special sense organs.

A course of lectures will be given for students of the Third and Fourth years. This course will consist of a systematic study of the regional anatomy of the human body as applied in the practice of medicine and surgery. The lectures will be illustrated by suitable preparations, and a series of demonstrations of landmarks will be conducted on the living subject.

Demonstrations.—A series of demonstrations will be conducted daily for students of the Second year. In this class the main facts in gross human anatomy will be demonstrated from recent dissections.

Dissection.—The dissecting-room will be open daily from 9 a.m. until 6 p.m. on Monday, Tuesday, Wednesday, Thursday and Friday, and from 9 a.m. till 12 noon on Saturday. Students will be required to conduct their work in a systematic manner and to conform to the regulations in force in the dissecting-room. One or more of the Assistant-Demonstrators will be in attendance at all times for the purpose of superintending the work of the students, and of giving instruction. Examinations will be conducted from time to time on the parts dissected, and marks allotted for the work done. Certificates for work in practical anatomy are granted to such students only as have obtained the requisite number of marks in the examinations.

The dissecting-room is admirably adapted for the purposes of practical anatomy. It is large and well ventilated, and is equipped in such a manner as to afford every possible com-

fort and convenience to the student. Each student is provided with a locker for his private use. A notable feature of
the dissecting-room is the excellent light, the room being
lighted from the roof through extensive sky-lights, and when
sunlight fails, electricity is employed with equally good
effect.

Museum.—In connection   dissecting-room a series
of preparations have been m   r the purpose of study.
The disarticulated bones of   on are included in this
collection, together with fro   s of the h   dy
wet preparations, illustratin   al anatomy,   o-
vided. A valuable and ins   series of St
of frozen s   s of Hi   hibited in
together wit   plete s   issections o
other prepa   Cur   series of
ing the topo   an   brai
Arrange   s   ul
from the os   t   h
a limited p

A pamp
guidance o
lations for
all studen

Professor o

Demonstra
Demonstr

The
tics of
various
channe
3. Die
also b
organ
mann
under
sible
Th
The fi

The work will be demc᷄. r ve in character. the student being familiarized with ᷄.. portant drugs and their preparations by daily demo᷄. ions in the class room. The demonstrations will inclu᷄l t important non-official as well as the official drugs.

The method of prepari᷄. z .e different groups of preparations, tinctures, ointments. ᷄u ositories, etc., will be shewn to the class as far as is pract a necessary.

The general principles ᷄ f osology, the factors modifving the doses of drugs will als I considered, and the writing of prescriptions with a view ᷄e practical application of the course.

The Second course of l t᷄es will be on the pharmacologi cal actions of the official ᷄n᷄ important non-official drugs.

A practical experime᷄. al ᷄ourse with special demonstra᷄ s will accompany the ab᷄᷄ lecture course. Each student ᷄᷄s have an opport᷄m᷄t to test for him᷄elf the pharma᷄ ᷄l action of some ᷄f ᷄e more important drugs. Th᷄ hus studied will in a᷄far as possible be typical of the ᷄ pharmacological gro᷄s.

᷄e Department posse᷄᷄ a very complete collection of ᷄ and prepared drug᷄. hese specimens are made u᷄e of iustrating the lecture ᷄n are displayed for inspection by students in suitable gla᷄ cases.

MEICINE.

rofessor of Medicine ᷄nd *Cnical Medicine*: A. McPHEDR᷄

᷄iate Professors of Medicine R. D. RUDOLF, J. T. FOTHERING᷄

Professor of ClinicalMedicine: J. L. DAVISON.

᷄ate Professors of Clinical ᷄edicine: ALLAN M. BAINES, W. P. CAVEN, W. ᷄ THISTLE, J. T. FOTHERINGHAM, A. R. GORDON, R. ᷄ DW᷄ER, H. B. ANDERSON.

᷄ates in Clinical Medici᷄e᷄ ᷄. BOYD, R. D. RUDOLF, G. CHAMBERS, H. C. PA᷄᷄S, W. GOLDIE.

᷄tors: D. McGILLIVRAY, T D. ARCHIBALD, G. W. HOWLAND.

᷄ese lectures are de᷄c᷄d to the consideration of the ᷄l principles of medi᷄ie and to the discussion of the

fort and convenience to the student. Each student is provided with a locker for his private use. A notable feature of the dissecting-room is the excellent light, the room being lighted from the roof through extensive sky-lights, and when sunlight fails, electricity is employed with equally good effect.

Museum.—In connection with the dissecting-room a series of preparations have been mounted for the purpose of study. The disarticulated bones of the skeleton are included in this collection, together with frozen sections of the human body; wet preparations, illustrating regional anatomy, are also provided. A valuable and instructive series of Steger's models of frozen sections of His are exhibited in the Museum, together with a complete series of dissections of the brain and other preparations. Cunningham's series of models illustrating the topographical anatomy of the brain are also exhibited.

Arrangements are such that a student may obtain bones from the osteological store-room, which he may take home for a limited period, if he so desire.

A pamphlet will be issued containing directions for the guidance of students of the class in anatomy, with the regulations for the dissecting-room. This should be procured by all students enrolled in the Anatomical Department.

MATERIA MEDICA AND THERAPEUTICS.

Professor of Materia Medica, Pharmacology and Therapeutics:
    J. M. MacCallum.
Demonstrator of Pharmacology: V. E. Henderson.
Demonstrator of Pharmacy: C. P. Lusk.

The course in therapeutics includes: 1. General therapeutics of the nature and action of remedies generally. 2. The various forms in which medicines are administered, and the channels through which they are introduced into the system. 3. Diet, hydrotherapy, massage, electricity and climate will also be dealt with. 4. Special therapeutics of the various organs of the body. This is treated in a practical and rational manner from the standpoint of the pathological conditions underlying disease, and will be accompanied in as far as possible by clinical demonstrations.

There will be two courses of lectures in the Second year. The first course will include Materia Medica and Pharmacy.

The work will be demonstrative in character, the student being familiarized with the important drugs and their preparations by daily demonstrations in the class room. The demonstrations will include the important non-official as well as the official drugs.

The method of preparing the different groups of preparations, tinctures, ointments, suppositories, etc., will be shewn to the class as far as is practically necessary.

The general principles of posology, the factors modifying the doses of drugs will also be considered, and the writing of prescriptions with a view to the practical application of the course.

The Second course of lectures will be on the pharmacological actions of the official and important non-official drugs.

A practical experimental course with special demonstrations will accompany the above lecture course. Each student will thus have an opportunity to test for himself the pharmacological action of some of the more important drugs. The drugs thus studied will in as far as possible be typical of the various pharmacological groups.

The Department possesses a very complete collection of crude and prepared drugs. These specimens are made use of in illustrating the lecture and are displayed for inspection by the students in suitable glass cases.

MEDICINE.

Professor of Medicine and Clinical Medicine: A. McPHEDRAN.

Associate Professors of Medicine: R. D. RUDOLF, J. T. FOTHERINGHAM.

Professor of Clinical Medicine: J. L. DAVISON.

Associate Professors of Clinical Medicine: ALLAN M. BAINES, W. P. CAVEN, W. B. THISTLE, J. T. FOTHERINGHAM, A. R. GORDON, R. J. DWYER, H. B. ANDERSON.

Associates in Clinical Medicine: G. BOYD, R. D. RUDOLF, G. CHAMBERS, H. C. PARSONS, W. GOLDIE.

Tutors: D. McGILLIVRAY, T. D. ARCHIBALD, G. W. HOWLAND.

These lectures are devoted to the consideration of the general principles of medicine and to the discussion of the internal diseases met with in this climate. When the subjects under consideration can be demonstrated to the whole class patients will be presented to illustrate the lectures. This method has been found of the greatest advantage. The wards and out-patient rooms of the several hospitals afford facilities for demonstrations to smaller classes. The lectures are also illustrated by lantern-slides, models, etc., from the Museum, and by morbid specimens from the Pathological Department.

The Third year class receives tutorial instructions in sections every week.

The teaching in Clinical Medicine is carried on at the Toronto General and St. Michael's Hospitals and the Victoria Hospital for Sick Children.

I.—THE STUDENTS OF THE THIRD YEAR are given instruction as follows:—

(1) In physical diagnosis, and methods of examining patients.

(2) In case-taking, they are required to report cases in the out-patient departments and wards of the hospitals.

(3) In the treatment of the more common diseases.

(4) A systematic course in clinical laboratory methods.

II.—THE GRADUATING CLASS will receive instruction as follows:—

(1) Clinical lectures in the hospital theatres.

(2) Clinical instruction in small classes in the wards of the hospitals.

(3) In preparing accurate histories and carrying out the requisite laboratory investigations of the cases assigned to them.

(4) Instruction in the various therapeutic means applicable to the cases under observation.

DISEASES OF CHILDREN.

This course comprises lectures to Third and Fourth year students on such subjects as diseases of the newly-born, infant feeding, diseases of the digestive system, the acute infectious diseases, etc. Daily clinics are held at the Hospital for Sick Children on medical and surgical cases in hospital.

PREVENTIVE MEDICINE.

Professor of Preventive Medicine, Didactic and Clinical: C. SHEARD

The course will consist of not more than 15 didactic and not less than 50 clinical lectures on the subject of Preventive Medicine, including instruction on the Exanthemata.

Contagion and infection, management of epidemics and quarantine will be dealt with.

SURGERY.

Professors of Surgery and Clinical Surgery:
> I. H. CAMERON, F. LeM. GRASETT, G. A. PETERS, L. TESKEY.

Associate Professor of Clinical Surgery and Clinical Anatomy:
> G. A. BINGHAM.

Associate Professors of Clinical Surgery:
> A. PRIMROSE, N. A. POWELL, W. OLDRIGHT, H. A. BRUCE, F. N. G. STARR.

Associate Professor of Clinical Surgery in Charge of Orthopædics:
> C. L. STARR.

Demonstrators in Clinical Surgery:
> W. MacKEOWN, C. A. TEMPLE, A. H. GARBATT.
> C. B. SHUTTLEWORTH, T. B. RICHARDSON, J. F. UREN.

This course of lectures comprehends:—

1. The general principles of surgery, as based upon what is known as: (*a*) The natural history of diseases of a surgical character as they affect the human frame, as, for example, abscess, ulceration, mortification, tumours, etc.; (*b*) The processes of repair and regeneration taking place in tissues, which have been diseased, such as the healing of wounds, the expulsion of foreign bodies, as bullets, dead bone, etc.; and (*c*) The part played in the economy by micro-organisms, involving a consideration of the germ theory of disease.

2. Surgical Injuries.

   (*a*) Of tissues, as fractures, dislocations, and injuries to nerves, blood vessels, etc.

   (*b*) Of organs contained in the so-called cavities of the body, the brain, lungs and abdominal viscera.

3. Surgical diseases, as aneurysm, varicose veins, calculus in the kidney or bladder, hernia, tuberculous disease of joints, bones, testicles, etc., pyæmia, erysipelas, etc.

4. The correction of malformations, deformities and defects, as club-foot, spinal curvatures, hare-lip, cleft-palate and other conditions usually classified under the headings of orthopædic and plastic surgery.

The course will be illustrated by plates and drawings, by specimens from the Museum and fresh specimens from the operating and post-mortem rooms, and by special reference to clinical cases falling under the immediate observation of the students in the wards of the Hospitals.

CLINICAL SURGERY.

In teaching clinical surgery, an effort is made to give as much personal instructions to each student as possible, and whenever it is practicable he is permitted to make a careful examination of the patients brought before the class.   In order to facilitate this the classes are made small, and are graded to some extent according to the degree of advancement of the students in their studies.   Whenever dressings are done and apparatus applied in the presence of the classes, each step of the proceeding is explained by the surgeon and the clinical clerks and dressers participate in the actual work.

During his course, each student has an opportunity of acting as clinical clerk and dresser, thus being afforded facilities for coming into that immediate contact with the patient which is so important from the point of view of practice, and which lends so much additional interest to the cases in his charge.

The material available for the instruction of students is abundant, consisting of out-door and in-door patients in the Toronto General Hospital, St. Michael's Hospital and the Hospital for Sick Children. In the last-named institution may be found cases, in great numbers and varieties, illustrating all the diseases, deformities and defects, such as club-foot, hare-lip, hip-joint disease, Pott's disease, and other conditions met with most frequently in the young.

A course of practical demonstrations in the technique of antiseptic surgery and wound treatment, the methods of surgical anæsthesia, general or local; the preparation and application of retentive apparatus in fractures, and allied subjects will be given to the Third year. Bandaging and other details of minor surgery will form a part of the course.

PATHOLOGY.

Professor of Pathology and Bacteriology and Curator of the Museum and Laboratories: J. J. MACKENZIE.

Associate-Professor of Pathology and Bacteriology: J. A. AMYOT.

Laboratory Assistant in Bacteriology: T. D. ARCHIBALD.

Demonstrators of Pathology:
  G. SILVERTHORN.
  C. J. WAGNER.

Assistant Demonstrators in Pathology:
  W. H. PEPLAR, H. C. PARSONS, M. M. CRAWFORD, F. A. CLARKSON, E. S. RYERSON, G. W. HOWLAND.

Assistants in Clinical Laboratory: M. H. V. CAMERON.

The course embraces lectures on general and special pathology, with demonstrations in gross morbid anatomy and pathological histology. The lectures to the Third year students will be mainly upon general pathology and bacteriology, and those to the students of the Fourth year, upon special pathology. Post-mortem examinations are performed by the Professor of Pathology at the General Hospital, and the students of the Fourth year will be expected to take part in these. Gross demonstrations are given in the Hospital mortuary and in the Pathological Laboratory, not only upon fresh material obtained from the hospitals, but upon materials obtained at other institutions in the city and upon specimens from the pathological museum.

The Pathological Laboratory is fully equipped with microscopes and other apparatus necessary for the study of pathological histology, and students of both years prepare and study about one hundred and fifty specimens of morbid tissue, the Third year students devoting their time to work in general pathology, whilst students of the Fourth year study the special pathological histology of the organs.

The clinical laboratories are under the charge of two assistants who are in constant attendance to give advice and instruction to students in their work in the examination of urine, blood, stomach contents, sputum, etc., and full records of the work of each student are preserved.

The pathological museum contains about two thousand specimens and is constantly growing, and students are given access to the cases and are expected to make as full use of the specimens as possible in their reading.

6

Classes in bacteriology are held every afternoon through-out the session, and the students of the Third year are sub-divided so as to give each student about eight weeks' con-tinuous work in the bacteriological laboratory.

HYGIENE.

Professor: W. Oldright.

The student is recommended to obtain from one of the works mentioned in the list of textbooks an elementary knowledge of the subject of each next succeeding lecture. The information thus obtained will be supplemented in the lectures, and fuller consideration given to these points which require special attention on account of differences of climate, population, occupations, social and political organisation, and other circumstances in Canada. Students are also guided in regard to sources of information and current literature relating to health work in this country. Visits are made to some outside institutions for practical demonstrations in sub-jects pertaining to Hygiene.

In addition to the theoretical teaching, practical demon-strations are given by means of various instruments and apparatus. The following subjects are embraced in the course: air, impurities and their effects, ventilation and heating; hygienic architecture; climatology: sewerage and disposal of refuse; water supplies; foods, dietaries; adulterations; occu-pations; physical and mental exercise and overwork; cloth-ing; baths; duties and functions of medical officers of health and boards of health; vital statistics; sanitary legislation—federal, provincial and municipal.

Museum of Hygiene.

The enlargement of the Museum of Hygiene and additions to the apparatus and samples for teaching and illustrating the various branches of Hygiene still continues, and exhibits con-tributed by manufacturers and other persons interested in the subject are being constantly added.

TOXICOLOGY.

Professor: W. H. ELLIS.

A series of lectures and demonstrations on toxicology is given under the following heads:—

THE NATURE OF POISONS.

Their properties, physical, chemical and physiological.

THE OCCURRENCE OF POISONS.

In nature, in the arts, and in common life. Danger from poisoning incidental to particular callings. Genesis of poisons in the dead and in the living body.

ANTIDOTES TO POISONS.

THE DETECTION OF POISONS.

Identification of poisons in the pure state. Separation from organic matter.

Post-mortem examinations for poisons.

MEDICAL JURISPRUDENCE.

Professor: N. A. POWELL.

The course will embrace *inter alia* a discussion of the medico-legal aspects of the following subjects:—

Medical evidence, ordinary and expert; inquests.

Thanatology—Signs of the reality of death; *post mortem* changes; autopsies and reports.

Presumption of death and of survivorship.

Personal identity of the living and of the dead.

Causes producing violent death, such as wounds, burns and scalds, heat or cold, lightning and electricity.

Strangulation, hanging, drowning, suffocation, starvation, feigned diseases, malingerings.

Medico-legal aspects of pregnancy.

Criminal abortion, infanticide, live birth, legitimacy, impotency and sterility.

Rape and allied offences against chastity.

Life assurance; medical ethics.

Civil and Criminal Malpractice.

MENTAL DISEASES.

Extra-Mural Professors: N. H. BEEMER, J. C. MITCHELL, C. K. CLARKE.

The course of lectures will be partly didactic, given in the lecture-rooms, and partly clinical, given at the Asylums. The subjects discussed will be altogether practical, and will embrace the following:—

1st. Definitions of terms in common use, and the reasons for their frequent misapplication.

2nd. Leading conditions in which a knowledge of mental diseases is necessary.

3rd. Groundwork of various classifications of mental diseases.

4th. Causes of mental diseases.

5th. Principal forms of mental diseases, with clinical illustrations.

6th. Special forms of mental diseases, with examples.

7th. Essential observations in making medical certificates, and methods of admittance to institutions.

8th. Treatment of various forms of mental diseases.

OBSTETRICS, GYNAECOLOGY AND PEDIATRICS.

Professor of Gynæcology and Operative Obstetrics:
J. ALGERNON TEMPLE.

Professor of Obstetrics: A. H. WRIGHT.

Professor of Gynæcology: J. F. W. ROSS.

Associate Professor of Obstetrics and Pediatrics: T. T. MACHELL.

Associate-Professor of Pediatrics: A. M. BAINES.

Associates in Obstetrics: K. C. McILWRAITH, F. FENTON.

There will be two separate courses in obstetrics; one for the students of the Third year in physiological obstetrics, and the other for students of the Fourth year in pathological obstetrics.

The Third year course in physiological obstetrics will include the following: anatomy and physiology of the female organs of reproduction; physiology of pregnancy; physiology, mechanism, and management of labour; management of the puerperal state; management of the infant.

The Fourth year course on pathological obstetrics will include: diseases of pregnancy, abortion and premature labour, dystocia, accidents before and after delivery, obstetrical operations, puerperal diseases, including septicæmia.

Practical demonstrations will be given on the phantom or cadaver, and diagrams, specimens, models, etc., will be used in illustrating the various subjects treated of in the two courses.

In the department of Gynæcology instruction will be given on the various methods of examination and diagnosis; the use and application of instruments; and the symptoms, diagnosis and treatment of diseases peculiar to women.

. The disorders of menstruation, leucorrhœa, chlorosis, metritis in its various forms, tumours, displacements and diseases of the uterus and ovaries, laceration of the cervix uteri and perineum, and abdominal surgery, will be treated of and illustrated by large plates, casts and morbid specimens in the didactic course, while operative gynæcology will be demonstrated in the Clinics in the Toronto General Hospital.

A special course of instruction in Disease in Children will be conducted by the Associate-Professor of Obstetrics and Pediatrics. He will be assisted in the clinical work by other members of the Faculty who are on the staff of the Hospital for Sick Children.

OPHTHALMOLOGY AND OTOLOGY.

Professors: R. A. REEVE, G. S. RYERSON, C. H. BURNHAM.
Associate-Professor: C. TROW.
Associate: J. M. McCALLUM.

In addition to a short course of didactic lectures on Diseases of the Eye and Ear at the University, practical instruction will be given four times in the week at the clinics in the Provincial (Mercer) Eye and Ear Infirmary, Toronto General Hospital.

LARYNGOLOGY AND RHINOLOGY.

Professor: G. R. McDONAGH.
Associate-Professor: D. J. GIBB WISHART.
Associate: GEOFFREY BOYD.

In the department of Larynology and Rhinology, a course of practical lectures on the commoner forms of disease of the Throat and Nose will be given, and in the General Hospital there will be clinical teaching and opportunities for examining patients on four afternoons each week.

THE TORONTO GENERAL HOSPITAL.   .

The following members of the Faculty are members of the staff of the Toronto General Hospital.

Consulting.

PROF. J. H. RICHARDSON, M.D.   PROF. C. SHEARD, M.D.
PROF. U. OGDEN, M.D.

Physicians.

PROF. A. McPHEDRAN, M.B.   PROF. J. L. DAVISON, M.D.
PROF. A. M. BAINES, M.D.   PROF. W. P. CAVEN, M.B.

Surgeons.

PROF. I. H. CAMERON, M.B.   PROF. G. A. PETERS, M.B.
PROF. F. LeM. GRASETT, M.B.   PROF. L. TESKEY.

Emergency Branch.

Surgeons.   Physicians.

PROF. G. BINGHAM, M.B.   PROF. J. M. MacCALLUM, M.D.
PROF. A. PRIMROSE, M.B.   PROF. J. T. FOTHERINGHAM, M.D.
PROF. N. A. POWELL, M.D.   PROF. W. B. THISTLE, M.B.
PROF. F. N. G. STARR, M.B.   PROF. A. R. GORDON, M.B.
PROF. H. A. BRUCE, M.B.   G. CHAMBERS, M.B.
A. H. GARRATT, M.B.   W. H. PEPLER, M.D.

Out-door.

Surgeons.   Physicians.

A. H. GARRATT, M.D.   PROF. A. R. GORDON, M.B.
C. A. TEMPLE, M.D.   PROF. R. D. RUDOLF, M.D.
PROF. C. L. STARR, M.B.   W. GOLDIE, M.B.
C. B. SHUTTLEWORTH, M.D.   J. W. O. MALLOCH, M.B.
W. H. PEPLER, M.D.   G. ELLIOTT, M.D.
    R. J. DWYER, M.D.

Gynæcology and Obstetrics.

PROF. J. ALGERTON TEMPLE, M.D.   PROF. A. H. WRIGHT, M.D.
PROF. J. F. W. ROSS, M.B.

Assistants in Obstetrics.

K. C. McILWRAITH, M.B.   F. FENTON, M.D.

Pathology.

PROF. J. J. McKENZIE, M.B.   H. C. PARSONS, M.D.
PROF. H. B. ANDERSON, M.D.   PROF. J. A. AMYOT, M.B.
W. GOLDIE, M.B.

Ophthalmology and Otology.

PROF. R. A. REEVE, M.D.   PROF. C. TROW, M.D.
PROF. G. S. RYERSON, M.D.   PROF. G. H. BURNHAM, M.D.

Rhinology and Laryngology.

PROF. G. R. McDONAGH, M.D.   PROF. D. J. GIBB WISHART, M.D.

Assistant in Rhinology and Laryngology.

G. BOYD, M.B.

Registrars.

G. W. HOWLAND, B.A., M.B.   F. W. MARLOW, M.D., C.M.

The Hospital has now 425 beds, and during the year the number of in-patients under treatment has varied from 250 to 300. During last year about 3,300 patients were admitted, and 16,000 patients received treatment in the out-door depart-ment.

All the patients in the Hospital are, as a rule, suffering from acute medical or surgical disease; the chronic cases are generally sent to the Home of Incurables or House of Provi-dence, and the convalescent patients are sent to the Convales-cent Home, recently enlarged on Well's Hill.

Clinical Training.

Clinical instruction is given in the various departments of the Hospital on all classes of patients.

I. *Theatre Lectures:*—Clinical Lectures are given on patients brought from the wards to the large theatre, by the professors of clinical medicine and of clinical surgery to the students of the Third and Fourth years.

II. *Instruction in the Wards:*—

(*a*) Medicine and Surgery:—A systematic course of bed-side instruction is given to a limited class of students. Ar-rangements are such that each physician and surgeon or his assistant is in daily attendance for the purpose of imparting instruction at the bedside. By this means provision is made for continuous daily work in the ward, and students of both Third and Fourth years are required to avail themselves of it.

(*b*) Gynæcology:—Small classes of students receive in-struction in diseases peculiar to women in the pavilion spe-cially devoted to the treatment of such patients. These classes meet twice a week. Increased facilities have recently been provided for an out-door gynæcological clinic.

(c) Obstetrics:—In the Burnside Lying-in Hospital, in which there are over 200 births a year, final students are permitted to witness and assist in the conduct of *labours*. Students are also allowed to make engagements with out-patients and to attend them in confinements at their own homes.

(d) Ophthalmology, Otology, Laryngology and Rhinology: —Diseases of the eye, ear, throat and nose are studied in the wards of the Andrew Mercer Infirmary.

III. *Surgical Operations*:—Surgical operations are performed in the large theatre every morning, or in cases of emergency at any time during the day or night when required. The theatre, which has recently been altered and enlarged, is capable of seating 600 students, and in the completeness of its arrangements is not excelled. The facilities afforded the students situated in all parts of the room for witnessing operations in all their details are unusually good.

IV. *Out-patient Clinics*:—The recent provision which has been made for the accommodation of out-patients will afford unsurpassed facilities for instruction in the important class of diseases which here pass under observation. A physician and a surgeon are in attendance daily, and the patients serve to illustrate the instruction. The cases presenting themselves in the special departments of the Hospital devoted to diseases of the eye, ear, etc., are available in the same manner. There will also be an out-door clinic in gynæcology.

V. *Pathology*:—

(a) Autopsies:—These are performed at stated hours by the Professor, or the Demonstrator of Pathology. The examinations are conducted in a systematic way, and instruction on the morbid conditions found is imparted to the students. The bearings of the gross post-mortem appearances on the conditions previously found at the bedside are carefully investigated, and, when necessary, arrangements are made for further examination, microscopical and chemical. There are about 200 autopsies during the year. Recently the theatre in which autopsies are made has been completely remodelled and every facility is provided for conducting the examinations. The light is excellent and the room capable of accommodating 150 students, (*b*) The examination and analysis of the various fluids, excreta and pathological products of patients in the wards, are conducted in the University Hospital laboratory. Students are required to keep systematic records of the results obtained by these examinations.

Clinical Clerks and Surgical Dressers.

Clinical clerks and surgical dressers are appointed to act for limited periods. They are required to take complete histories of cases allotted to them, and to receive certificates for the same, as required by the Ontario Medical Council. Postmortem clerks are appointed, and are required to make complete reports of all autopsies made in the post-mortem room, which is situated in the Hospital grounds. Clinical clerks and surgical dressers are also appointed in the departments of gynæcology, ophthalmology and otology.

Every student in the Department of Surgery shall be required to take the history, attend the dressing and keep the record of six cases in the Ward.

If any such case come to operation he shall attend the same, disinfect himself, don an operating gown and come within the pale of the theatre to render such assistance as may be required of him, and to record the facts of the operation and the result. If any such come to post-mortem examination he shall attend the same, render such assistance as may be required of him and record the findings.

Students in Clinical Medicine shall be required to observe this last regulation respecting attendance at post-mortem examinations.

Resident Assistants in the Hospital.

Five resident assistants are appointed annually from the graduates in medicine of the University, and hold their positions for one year. They will have full opportunities for acquiring experience in the general and special wards of the Hospital, and during the session they will have charge under the physicians and surgeons in the general wards.

The Appointment of Students of the Fifth Year.

Certain junior positions on the House Staff of the Toronto General Hospital will be available for students in the Fifth Year, and selection of suitable men for these positions will be made in a similar manner to that adopted in connection with the Senior House Appointments. Any candidate wishing to apply for such position should make formal application to the Hospital authorities, addressing his communication to the Secretary of the Toronto General Hospital. In addition to this he should forward his name to the Secretary of the Faculty of Medicine indicating that he is an applicant for appointment. The appointment will be made by the Hospital authorities on the recommendation of the Faculty of Medicine.

HOUSE STAFF.

Resident Pathologist.
A. H. W. CAULFEILD, M.B.

INTERNS:

W. A. BURR, M.D.
G. B. ARCHER, M.B.
A. G. McPHEDRAN, B.A., M.B.
E. C. BURSON, M.B.
F. J. BRODIE, M.D.
A. H. ADAMS, B.A., M.B.
K. H. VANNORMAN, M.B.

A. McNALLY, M.B.
T. A. DAVIES, M.B.
F. W. ROLPH, B.A., M.D., C.M.
J. H. SOADY, M.B.
F. J. BULLER, M.B.
J. H. KIDD, M.D., C.M.

EXTERNS:

C. W. MURRAY, M.B.
H. CLENDINNING, M.D., C.M.
G. STEWART, M.B.

A. J. GILCHRIST. M.B.
D. McKENZIE, M.B.
A. G. WALLIS, M.B.

HOSPITAL FOR SICK CHILDREN.

The following members of the Faculty are members of the Hospital staff:—

PROF. U. OGDEN, M.D.
PROF. J. W. F. ROSS.

PROF. C. SHEARD, M.D.

Physicians.

PROF. A. McPHEDRAN, M.B.
PROF. A. M. BAINES, M.D.
PROF. H. T. MACHELL, M.B.

PROF. J. T. FOTHERINGHAM, M.D.
PROF. W. B. THISTLE, M.D.
PROF. H. B. ANDERSON, M.D.

Surgeons.

PROF. I. H. CAMERON, M.B.
PROF. G. A. BINGHAM, M.D.
PROF. A. PRIMROSE, M.B.

PROF. G. A. PETERS, M.B.
PROF. N. A. POWELL, M.D.
PROF. CLARENCE L. STARR, M.B.

Ophthalmology and Otology.

PROF. R. A. REEVE, M.D.
PROF. C. TROW, M.B.

PROF. J. M. MacCALLUM, M.D.

Rhinology and Laryngology.

PROF. G. R. McDONAGH.   PROF. D. J. GIBB WISHART.

Physician to the Infectious Wards.

W. GOLDIE, M.B.

Pathologists.

W. H. PEPLER, M.D.   W. J. O. MALLOCH, M.B.

Bacteriologist.

W. GOLDIE, M.B.

Out-door and Assistant.

PROF. F. N. G. STARR, M.B.   H. C. PARSONS, M.B.
PROF. R. D. RUDOLF, M.D., C.M. G. BOYD, M.B.
C. B. SHUTTLEWORTH, M.B.

Anæsthetist.

J. A. S. GRAHAM, M.B.

This large Hospital, with 160 beds, is entirely devoted to disease in children. In the clinics cases exemplifying the various diseases in infancy and childhood will be exhibited. Abundant opportunities for a personal examination of all cases will be afforded.

Resident assistants are appointed annually from the graduates in medicine of the University, and hold their position for the year. The opportunity thus afforded for obtaining a practical knowledge of this very important department of medical practice is unsurpassed.

For the year 1905-6 they were:—

W. W. WRIGHT, M.B.   A. C. BENNETT, M.B.
G. D. R. BLACK, M.B.   G. R. STRATHY, M.D., C.M.

ST. MICHAEL'S HOSPITAL.

The following members of the Faculty are members of the staff of St. Michael's Hospital:—

Physicians.

PROF. A. McPHEDRAN, M.D.   PROF. R. J. DWYER, M.B.
PROF. H. B. ANDERSON, M.D.

Physician and Dermatologist.

GRAHAM CHAMBERS, M.B.

Surgeons.

PROF. I. H. CAMERON, M.B.   PROF. H. A. BRUCE, M.B.
PROF. A. PRIMROSE, M.B.   PROF. G. A. BINGHAM, M.B.
PROF. W. OLDRIGHT, M.D.   W. MacKEOWN, M.B.
PROF. H. W. AIKINS, M.B.   J. F. UREN, M.D.

Gynæcologist.

PROF. J. F. W. ROSS, M.B.

Assistant Obstetrician.

K. C. McILWRAITH, M.B..

Rhinology and Laryngology.

PROF. D. J. GIBB WISHART, M.D.

Assistant.

G. BOYD, M.B.

Pathologist.

PROF. J. A. AMYOT, M.B.

Assistant Surgeons.

C. A. TEMPLE, M.D.   F. W. MARLOW, M.B.
A. H. GARRATT, M.D.   G. SILVERTHORN, M.B.

Ophthalmology and Otology.

PROF. J. M. MacCALLUM, M.D.

Out-door Staff.

M. M. CRAWFORD, M.B.   P. W. O'BRIEN, M.B.
W. J. McCOLLUM, M.B.   C. B. SHUTTLEWORTH, M.B.

This institution is conducted as a General Hospital; where medical, surgical and obstetrical cases are admitted. The number of patients admitted last year was about 1,500. The accommodation has recently been enlarged by the addition of a new wing, so that there are now 160 beds. An operating theatre has been provided, constructed with all the necessary modern equipment for the practice of antiseptic surgery.

Clinical instruction is given in this Hospital by those members of the staff who are also on the teaching staff of the University of Toronto. Opportunity is also provided for the study of Pathology. Post-mortem examinations are conducted systematically so that students may avail themselves of the material in this department. Clinical clerks and surgical dressers are appointed from the students in attendance at the Hospital.

Resident assistants are appointed annually from the graduates in Medicine of the University of Toronto.

For the current year they are:—

G. H. RICHARDS.   W. CHAMBERS.
J. F. L. KILLORAN.   F. J. SHEAHAN.

TEXTBOOKS.

Disease in Children:—Holt, $6; Goodhart and Still, $3.50; Koplick, $4; Dawson Williams, $3.50; Taylor and Wells, $4.

Medicine:—Osler, ($5.50) for the 4th year; Munro, ($3.75) Maybe for the third year; Strümpell, $6.

Diagnosis:—Sahli's Diagnostic Methods, $ ...

Clinical Medicine:—Hutchison & Rainy.

Dermatology:—Crocker, $4.50; Stelwagon, $5.

Hygiene:—Parkes and Kenwood, $3; Egbert, $2.25; Wilson, $3; Harrington's *Practical Hygiene*, $4.25. For reference—Bergey, $3; Stevenson and Murphy, vols. 1 and 2, $12; DeChaumont's *Parkes*, $4; Abbott's Hygiene of Transmissible Disease, $2.50; Principles of Sanitary Science and *Public* Health, Sedgwick's $3; Thresh on Water Supplies, $2.

Mental Diseases:—Daniel Clark, $1.25; T. S. Clouston, $4.50; Henry J. Berkley, $5; Brower-Bannister, $2.

Anatomy:—Cunningham's Text Book, $6; Morris, $6; Gray, $6.25; Quain; Cunningham's Practical Anatomy, 2 vols., $5; Ellis's Demonstrations of Anatomy, edited by Thane, $3.75; Brodie's Atlas of Dissections, Illustrated, 4 vols., $9.50; Anatomy and *Physiology* of the Nervous System, L. F. Barker, $5; Deaver's Surgical Anatomy, $30; Embryology, Heisler, $2.50; Anatomy of the Nervous System, Edinger, $3; Told's Human Anatomy. Hand Atlas of Human Anatomy; Spalteholtz, translated by Barker, $18; Schultze's "Atlas of Topographical Anatomy."

Physiology:—Foster, vols., $9; New American Edition, 1 vol., ;
Howell, Text Book of Physiology, $6; Waller, $4; Stewa
$3.75; Brodie Essentials of Experimental Physiology, $1.7
Text Book o Physiology, edited by E. A. Schäfer, 2 v
$18; Lee's ext Book of Physiology, $4; Chapman's Ph
siology, $4.25 Kirk's Physiology, edited by Halliburton (Er
lish edition), $3.

Histology:—Böhm, v. Davidoff and Huber, Text Book of Histolog;
2nd ed., $3.5; Szymonowicz and MacCallum, Text Book
Histology an Microscopic Anatomy, $4.75; Sobotta a
Huber, Hand Atlas of Human Histology and Microscop
Anatomy, $4.0. Text Book of Histology—Bailey.

Embryology:—Minot Iuman Embryology; Minot, Laboratory Tex
Book of Embryology; McMurrich, Manual of Embryology.

Chemistry:—Remsen ollege Chemistry, $2, or Newth, Inorganic Chem
istry: Remsey Organic Chemistry, $1.25. Other books o
reference recommended: Bloxam's Chemistry (Inorganic an
Organic: Ruter, Inorganic Chemistry, $1.75; Hills, Chem
istry for Students of Medicine, $3, Bernthsen's Organi
Chemistry su, 59.

Pharmacology and Parmacy:—Cushny, Pharmacology, $3.75; Soll
mann, Pharmacology, $3.75; Mitchell Bruce, Materia Medica
and Therapeuics, $1.50; Heebner's Synopsis, $1.50.

Therapeutic —Yeo's Jlinical Therapeutics, 2 vols., $5.00; Hare's
Practical Theapentics, $4.00; Lauder Brunton, On the Action
of Medicines.

Surgery:—Principles c Surgery, Nancrede, $2.00; Erichsen, 2 vols.,
$11; Walsham $3; Treves' System, 2 vols., $12; Treves' Sur
gical Operation, $2; American Text Book of Surgery, $7;
Manual of Surgery, Rose and Carless; Jacobson, The Operations
of Surgery, $5 Operative Surgery, Bickham; Wharton's Band
aging and Mnor Surgery, $3; Kocher's Operative Surgery,
$5, Operative Surgery, Bryant, 2 vols.; Surgery, by Ameri
can Author, Roswell Park, $7; Kelly, Diseases of the Ap
pendix, $5.0; White and Martin, on Genito-Urinary Diseases,
$6.50; Genit Urinary and Venereal Diseases, Taylor;
Trauma:i Injuries of the Brain, Phelps, $5; Fractures and
Di-locations, timson, $5; Fractures, Scudder, $5; Fractures,
Hogane, $4; J. Clark, on Orthopædic Surgery, $5; Fox's
Atlas of Ski Diseases, $24; Genito-Urinary Diseases, Lyd
ston, $5; American Text Book of Genito-Urinary Diseases,
$7; Syphilis nd Venereal Diseases, Hyde and Montgomery,
$4; International Clinics, $9; Bergmann and Mikulicz's Sur
gery, $5; Esmarch's Surgical Technique, $7; Mayo Robson
on Diseases o the Stomach, $4; Moynihan, Gall-Stones, $4;

Robson on Gall-Bladder, $4; Ick's Surgical Asepsis, $1.25; Röntgen Rays, Pusey-Caldwell $5; Orthopædic Surgery, Bradford and Lovett; Whitman Orthopedic Surgery, $5.50; Albert, Surgical Diagnosis, $3.50; Principles of Surgery, Lenz, J. Jackson Clarke; Rectum, Gant; American Practice of Surgery, Bryant & Buck, 8 vols.; The Reference Handbook of Medical Sciences.

Midwifery:—The Practice of Obstetrics by American authors, edited by Jewett, $5; American Text book of Obstetrics, edited by Norris, $7; Obstetrics, Adam Wright, $4.50; Whitridge Williams, $6; Lusk, $5; Hirst, 6; Galabin, $4; Evans, $3 Jellett, $3; Fothergill, $3; Clinical Obstetrics, Jardine, $3.75 Edgar, Obstetrics, $6; Disease of Women, MacNaughton-Jones; Practical Obstetrics, Grand & Jarman.

Gynæcology:—Galabin, $2.25; Garrigues $4; Hart and Barbour, $5; Pozzi, 2 vols., $12; Allbutt and Playfair, a System of Gynæcology, $6; Hermann, $5; Kelly Oper. Gynæcol., 2 vols., $15; Cancer and Uterus, Cullen; Daley $6, Penrose, $3.75; C. A. L. Reed; Gilliam, $4; Dough, Diseases of Abdomen.

Pathology:—Ziegler, General, 1 vol., $5.; Special, 2 vols., $8.00; Delafield & Pruden, 7th edition, $5; American Text Book of Pathology, $7.50; Coplin, Manual o Pathology, fourth edition, $3.50; Mallory & Wright, Pathological Technique, 3rd edition, $3.

Bacteriology:—Muir & Ritchie, $3.75; Abott, $2.75.

Clinical Methods:—Hutchinson & Rain Clinical Methods, $2.50; Crofton, Clinical Urinology, $2.5 Simon, Clinical Diagnosis, by Microscopical and Chemical Methods, 5th edition, $4.

Medical Jurisprudence:—Reese, $3; American Text Book of Legal Medicine, Petersen and Haines, 10; Draper, Legal Medicine, $4; Herald, $4; Mann, $4; Luff, 5; Vivian Poore, $4; Taylor, $4.50. References: Whitthaus and Becker, $20; McLane Hamilton, $11; Greene, Life Insurance, $4; The Physician Himself, Cathell (13th ed.).

Anæsthesia:—Hewitt, $4; Probyn-William $1.25; Patton, $2.

Biology:—Parker, $2.60; Huxley, $2.60.

Physics:—Gage's Principles of Physics, $1.30.

Ophthalmology:—Nettleship, $2.25; Swazy, $3; Juler, $5.50; de Schweinitz, $5; Carter and Fra, $2.25; J. Edward Jackson, $2.50; May, $2; Posey and 'right, Diseases of the Eye, Ear, Nose and Throat, $7; May Diseases of the Eye, $2; Vesey, Diseases of the Eye, $2.

Otology:—Pritchard's, $1.50; Field, $3.75 Buck, $2; Roosa, $5.25; B   anual of Otology, $2.

Laryngolo   ' Brown, $8; Bosworth, $4.50; Price Brown,

Physiology:—Foster, 4 vols., $9; New American Edition, 1 vol., $5; Howell, Text Book of Physiology, $6; Waller, $4; Stewart, $3.75; Brodie, Essentials of Experimental Physiology, $1.75; Text Book of Physiology, edited by E. A. Schäfer, 2 vols., $18; Hall's Text Book of Physiology, $4; Chapman's Physiology, $4.25; Kirk's Physiology, edited by Halliburton (English edition), $3.

Histology:—Böhm, v. Davidoff and Huber, Text Book of Histology, 2nd ed., $3.50; Szymonowicz and MacCallum, Text Book of Histology and Microscopic Anatomy, $4.75; Sobotta and Huber, Hand Atlas of Human Histology and Microscopic Anatomy, $4.50. Text Book of Histology—Bailey.

Embryology:—Minot, Human Embryology; Minot, Laboratory Text Book of Embryology; McMurrich, Manual of Embryology.

Chemistry:—Remsen College Chemistry, $2, or Newth, Inorganic Chemistry; Remsen, Organic Chemistry, $1.25. Other books of reference recommended: Bloxam's Chemistry (Inorganic and Organic); Richter, Inorganic Chemistry, $1.75; Hills, Chemistry for Students of Medicine, $3, Bernthsen's Organic Chemistry sup., 59.

Pharmacology and Pharmacy:—Cushny, Pharmacology, $3.75; Sollmann, Pharmacology, $3.75; Mitchell Bruce, Materia Medica and Therapeutics, $1.50; Heebner's Synopsis, $1.50.

Therapeutics:—Yeo's Clinical Therapeutics, 2 vols., $5.00; Hare's Practical Therapeutics, $4.00; Lauder Brunton, On the Action of Medicines.

Surgery:—Principles of Surgery, Nancrede, $2.00; Erichsen, 2 vols., $11; Walsham, $3; Treves' System, 2 vols., $12; Treves' Surgical Operations, $2; American Text Book of Surgery, $7; Manual of Surgery, Rose and Carless; Jacobson, The Operations of Surgery, $3; Operative Surgery, Bickham; Wharton's Bandaging and Minor Surgery, $3; Kocher's Operative Surgery, $5; Operative Surgery, Bryant, 2 vols.; Surgery, by American Authors, Roswell Park, $7; Kelly, Diseases of the Appendix, $10; White and Martin, on Genito-Urinary Diseases, $6.50; Genito-Urinary and Venereal Diseases, Taylor; Traumatic Injuries of the Brain, Phelps, $5; Fractures and Dislocations, Stimson, $5; Fractures, Scudder, $5; Fractures, Hopkins, $4; J. Clark, on Orthopædic Surgery, $5; Fox's Atlas of Skin Diseases, $24; Genito-Urinary Diseases, Lydston, $5; American Text Book of Genito-Urinary Diseases, $7; Syphilis and Venereal Diseases, Hyde and Montgomery, $4; International Clinics, $9; Bergmann and Mikulicz's Surgery, $3; Esmarch's Surgical Technique, $7; Mayo Robson on Diseases of the Stomach, $4; Moynihan, Gall-Stones, $4;

Robson on Gall-Bladder, $4; Beck's Surgical Asepsis, $1.25; Röntgen Rays, Pusey-Caldwell, $5; Orthopædic Surgery, Bradford and Lovett; Whitman, Orthopedic Surgery, $5.50; Albert, Surgical Diagnosis, $3.50; Principles of Surgery, Lenn, J. Jackson Clarke; Rectum, Gant; American Practice of Surgery, Bryant & Buck, 8 vols.; The Reference Handbook of Medical Sciences.

Midwifery:—The Practice of Obstetrics, by American authors, edited by Jewett, $5; American Text Book of Obstetrics, edited by Norris, $7; Obstetrics, Adam Wright, $4.50; Whitridge Williams, $6; Lusk, $5; Hirst, $5; Galabin, $4; Evans, $3; Jellett, $3; Fothergill, $3; Clinical Obstetrics, Jardine, $3.75; Edgar, Obstetrics, $6; Diseases of Women, MacNaughton-Jones; Practical Obstetrics, Grandid & Jarnian.

Gynæcology:—Galabin, $2.25; Garrigues, $4; Hart and Barbour, $5; Pozzi, 2 vols., $12; Allbutt and Playfair, a System of Gynæcology, $6; Hermann, $5; Kelly, Oper. Gynæcol., 2 vols., $15; Cancer and Uterus, Cullen; Dudley, $5; Penrose, $3.75; C. A. L. Reed; Gilliam, $4; Douglas, Diseases of Abdomen.

Pathology:—Ziegler, General, 1 vol., $5.; Special, 2 vols., $8.00; Delafield & Pruden, 7th edition, $5; American Text Book of Pathology, $7.50; Coplin, Manual of Pathology, fourth edition, $3.50; Mallory & Wright, Pathological Technique, 3rd edition, $3.

Bacteriology:—Muir & Ritchie, $3.75; Abbott, $2.75.

Clinical Methods:—Hutchinson & Rainy, Clinical Methods, $2.50; Crofton, Clinical Urinology, $2.50; Simon, Clinical Diagnosis, by Miscroscopical and Chemical Methods, 5th edition, $4.

Medical Jurisprudence:—Reese, $3; American Text Book of Legal Medicine, Petersen and Haines, $10; Draper, Legal Medicine, $4; Herald, $4; Mann, $4; Luff, $6; Vivian Poore, $4; Taylor, $4.50. References: Whitthaus and Becker, $20; McLane Hamilton, $11; Greene, Life Insurance, $4; The Physician Himself, Cathell (13th ed.).

Anæsthesia:—Hewitt, $4; Probyn-Williams, $1.25; Patton, $2.

Biology:—Parker, $2.60; Huxley, $2.60.

Physics:—Gage's Principles of Physics, $1.30.

Ophthalmology:—Nettleship, $2.25; Swanzy, $3; Juler, $5.50; de Schweinitz, $5; Carter and Frost, $2.25; J. Edward Jackson, $2.50; May, $2; Posey and Wright, Diseases of the Eye, Ear, Nose and Throat, $7; May, Diseases of the Eye, $2; Vesey, Diseases of the Eye, $2.

Otology:—Prichard's, $1.50; Field, $3.75; Buck, $2; Roosa, $5.25; Bacon's Manual of Otology, $2.

Laryngology:—Lennox Brown, $8; Bosworth, $4.50; Price Brown, $3.50; Coakley, $2.75.

Time Table, Session 1905-1906.
FIRST YEAR.

	MONDAY.	TUESDAY.	WEDNESDAY.	THURSDAY.	FRIDAY.	
9-10 a.m.	†Physics	Pract. Biology. (A) †Pract. Physics. (B) *Pract. Physiology. (B)	†Pract. Physics. (B) *Pract. Physiology (B)	†Pract. Physics. (A) *Pract. Physiology. (A)	Pract. Biology. (B) †Pract. Physics. (A) *Pract. Physiology. (A)	Practical
10-11 a.m.	Biology.	Pract. Biology. (A) †Pract. Physics. (B) *Pract. Physiology. (B)	†Pract. Physics. (B) *Pract. Physiology. (B)	†Pract. Physics. (A) *Pract. Physiology. (A)	Pract. Biology. (B) †Pract. Physics. (A) *Pract. Physiology. (A)	Practical
11-12 m.	Anatomy.	Chemistry.	*Physiology.	Biology.	Anatomy.	*Physiolo
12-1 p.m.		†Physics.	Chemistry.	†Physics.		
1-2 p.m.						
2-3 p.m.	Practical Anatomy.	Pract. Chemistry. (A) Pract. Anatomy. (B)	Biology.	Pract. Chemistry. (B) Pract. Anatomy. (A)	Practical Anatomy.	
3-4 p.m.	Practical Anatomy.	Pract. Chemistry. (A) Pract. Anatomy. (B)	Practical Anatomy.	Pract. Chemistry. (B) Pract. Anatomy. (A)	Practical Anatomy.	
4-5 p.m.	Practical Anatomy.	Pract. Chemistry. (A) Pract. Anatomy. (B)	Practical Anatomy.	Pract. Chemistry. (B) Pract. Anatomy. (A)	Practical Anatomy.	

† Michaelmas Term only   * Easter Term only

E

MONDAY.	TUESDAY.	WEDNESDAY.	THURSDAY.	FRIDAY.	SATURDAY.
Materia Medica.		Materia Medica.			
Pract. Histology. (A)	*Embryology.	Pract. Histology. (A)	Pract. Histology. (B)	Practical Physiology.	Practical Physiology.
Pract. Histology. (A)	Physiology.	Pract. Histology. (A)	Pract. Histology. (B)	Practical Physiology.	Practical Physiology.
Physiology.	Anatomy.	Anatomy.	Physiology.	Practical Physiology.	Practical Physiology.
Chemistry.	Pharmacology.	Physiology.	Anatomy.	Chemistry.	Anatomy.
Pract. Anatomy. (A) Pract. Chemistry. (B)	*Histology. (A) †Practical Anatomy. (B)	Practical Anatomy.	†Histology. *Embryology.	Pract. Histology. (B) Pract. Chemistry. (A)	
Pract. Anatomy. (A) Pract. Chemistry. (B)	Practical Anatomy. (A) (B)	Practical Anatomy.	Practical Anatomy.	Pract. Histology. (B) Pract. Chemistry. (A)	
Pract. Anatomy. (A) Pract. Chemistry. (B)	Practical Anatomy. (A) (B)	Practical Anatomy.	Practical Anatomy.	Pract. Chemistry. (A)	

†Histology Lectures during Michaelmas Term only.

*Embryology Lectures during Easter Term only.

THIRD YEAR.

	MONDAY.	TUESDAY.	WEDNESDAY.	THURSDAY.	FRIDAY.	
8-9 a.m.						Diseases of
9-10 a.m.						Pathological logy Demon
10-11 a.m.						Pathological logy Demon
11-12 m.	Jurisprudence.	General Pathology.	Obstetrics.	Medicine. (Third Year lecture theatre).	General Pathology.	Clinical I Methods
12-1 p.m.						
1-2 p.m.	Clinical Laboratory Methods.	Topographical Anatomy.	Clinical Laboratory Methods.	Topographical Anatomy.	Toxicology.	
2-3 p.m.	Medicine. (Third Year lecture theatre).	Therapeutics.	Medicine. (Third Year lecture theatre).	*Therapeutics. †Gross Pathology.	Pathological Histology Demonstrations.	
3-4 p.m.	Surgery.	Obstetrics.	Surgery.	*Jurisprudence. †Gross Pathology.	Pathological Histology Demonstrations.	
4-5.30 p.m.	Bacteriology.	Bacteriology.	Bacteriology.	Bacteriology.	Bacteriology.	

FOURTH YEAR.

	MONDAY.	TUESDAY.	WEDNESDAY.	THURSDAY.	FRIDAY.	
8-9 a.m.						Obs
9-10 a.m.						Obste
10-11 a.m.						
11-12 m.						Hygie
12-1 p.m.						
1-2 p.m.	Special Pathology.	Pathological Histology.	Special Pathology.	Obstetrics.		
2-3 p.m.	Medicine.	Pathological Histology.	Medicine.	Pathological Histology.	Obstetrics.	
3-4 p.m.	Surgery.	Gynaecology.	Surgery.	Pathological Histology.	Gynaecology.	
4-5 p.m.						
5-6 p.m.	Ophthalmology. Otology. Laryngology.			Preventive Medicine.		

*Easter Term only.　　†Michaelmas Term only.

FIFTII YEAR.

	MONDAY.	TUESDAY.	WEDNESDAY.	THURSDAY.	FRIDAY.
9-10 a.m.	†Special Pathology.	Medicine and Clinical Medicine. T. G. H.	Special Pathology.	Medicine and Clinical Medicine. T. G. H.	Surgery and Clinical Surgery. T. G. H. Anaesthetics. (2 Months beginning January 5, 1906). T. G. H. (Dr. Anderson).
10-11 a.m.	†Special Pathology.	Medicine and Clinical Medicine. T. G. H.	Special Pathology.	Medicine and Clinical Medicine. T. G. H.	Surgery and Clinical Surgery. T. G. H.
11-12 a.m.	†Special Pathology.	Medicine and Clinical Medicine. T. G. H.	Special Pathology.	Medicine and Clinical Medicine. T. G. H.	Surgery and Clinical Surgery. T. G. H.
12-2 p.m.					
2-3 p.m.	Operations on the Cadaver. (About 6 weeks beginning January 8, 1906).	Operations on the Cadaver. (About 6 weeks beginning January 8, 1906).	Operations on the Cadaver. (About 6 weeks beginning January 8, 1906).	Operations on the Cadaver. (About 6 weeks beginning January 8, 1906).	Advanced Physiology. (Easter Term).

FIFTH YEAR.—Continued.

3-4 p.m.	Special Therapeutics. (Michaelmas Term).	Laryngology and Rhinology. T. G. H. (Dr. McDonagh). (Michaelmas Term). *Ophthalmology and Otology. T. G. H. (Dr. Reeve). (Easter Term).	Regional Anatomy. (Easter Term).	*Ophthalmology and Otology. T. G. H. (Dr. Trow).	Laryngology and Rhinology. H. S. C. (Dr. Wishart).
4-5 p.m.	Operative Obstetrics.			Clinical Gynæcology.	Life Assurance. (6 Weeks beginning January 5, 1906). History of Medicine. (6 Weeks beginning February 16, 1906).
5-6 p.m.					

NOTE.—Students of the Fifth Year may be required to do Special Work in any of the Subjects of Study at other hours than those on the Time Table. Students are required to attend and assist in Autopsies at the Toronto General Hospital. The hours for su posted from time to time on the Bulletin Board at the University. Clinical laboratory work must be carried on in connection witl seen in the clinics.

*These clinics will not be given in the 6 weeks during which the student is engaged in operations on the Cadaver.

†This course will include surgical Pathology and the Pathology of the central nervous system.

THE DISSECTING ROOM   Eastern Half.

THE UNIVERSITY OF TORONTO MEDICAL SOCIETY.

This Society consists of the graduates and undergraduates enrolled in the Faculty of Medicine of the University of Toronto. It is under the patronage of the members of the Medical Faculty and its object is to deal with all matters pertaining to the general interest and welfare of the students, specially:—

(*a*) To encourage interest in general medical science and literature, and in the pursuit of medical studies.

(*b*) To provide a supply of periodicals and magazines for the reading rooms.

(*c*) To be a means of communication between the Student body and the Faculty or others, when such communication is desirable.

UNIVERSITY OF TORONTO MEDICAL STUDENTS' YOUNG MEN'S CHRISTIAN ASSOCIATION.

The meetings are held weekly in the building of the Young Men's Christian Association. The clergy and other prominent residents of the city frequently take part in the proceedings.

The objects of the association are to form a bond of union between medical students whose principles and aim in life are "Christian," and to render whatever practical assistance is possible to all medical students, especially those who are entering upon their medical studies. The Reception Committee of the association will be at the Union Station to meet and welcome all incoming students and to give any information and assistance that may be required. A list of suitable boarding houses will be available for the convenience of those who require it.

REGULATIONS RELATING TO STUDENTS.

1. No student will be registered in any year, or be allowed to continue in attendance, whose presence for any cause is deemed by the University Council to be prejudicial to the interests of the University. Registration in any year does not entitle a student to Registration in a subsequent year.

2. Students are required to attend the courses of instruction and the examinations in all subjects prescribed for students of their respective standing, and no student will be permitted to remain in the University who persistently neglects academic work.

3. All interference on the part of any student with the personal liberty of another, by arresting him, or summoning him to appear before any tribunal of students, or otherwise subjecting him to any indignity or personal violence, is forbidden by the Council. Any student convicted of participation in such proceedings will render himself liable to expulsion from the University.

4. A student who is under suspension, or who has been expelled from a College or the University, will not be admitted to the University buildings or grounds.

5. The constitution of every University society or association of students and all amendments to any such constitution must be submitted for approval to the University Council. All programmes of such societies or associations must, before publication, receive the sanction of the Council. Permission to invite any person not a member of the Faculty of the University to preside at or address a meeting of any society or association must be similarily obtained. Societies and associations are required to confine themselves to the objects laid down in their constitution.

6. The name of the University is not to be used in connection with a publication of any kind without the permission of the University Council.

Faculty of Medicine.

MATRICULATION.

General Regulations.

Candidates may enter the Faculty of Arts by passing either the Junior or the Senior Matriculation examination.

Candidates for Junior Matriculation must produce satisfactory certificates of good character and of having completed the sixteenth year of their age.

The subjects of Junior Matriculation are as follows:—Latin, English, History, Mathematics, and any two of the following: Greek, German, French, Experimental Science. In view of the Language requirements in the Undergraduate course, candidates are strongly recommended to take two languages for their options.

Pass and honour papers will be set in each of these subjects.

The pass papers are as follows:—Latin Authors, Latin Composition; English Grammar, English Composition, English Literature; History; Arithmetic, Algebra, Euclid; Greek Authors, Greek Composition; German Authors, German Composition; French Authors, French Composition; Experimental Science.

The pass standard in each subject is thirty-three per cent. of the marks assigned thereto.

The first class honour standard is seventy-five per cent.; the second class sixty-six per cent., and the third class fifty per cent. of the marks assigned to the subject.

Candidates for honours and scholarships will be examined only on the honour papers in a subject, but candidates who fail to obtain honours may receive pass standing in the subject.

Candidates who have obtained pass standing in at least one-half of the subjects may complete Junior Matriculation by passing in the remaining subjects at a subsequent examination or examinations.

The examination for pass and honour Junior Matriculation is held annually in July at centres in Ontario, and, if application is made to the Senate, the examination may, with the co-operation of the Department of Education, be held at centres outside Ontario.

Applications accompanied by the prescribed fee must be sent not later than the 24th of May to the local Public School Inspector, or in the case of candidates intending to write at the University, to the Registrar.

Scholarship candidates must also send a special application by the same date to the Registrar according to a form to be obtained from him. This application must be accompanied by the fee when the candidate intends to write at the University; when he proposes to write at some other centre, the ordinary application and the fee must be sent to the local Public School Inspector.

A Junior Matriculation examination will be held in June at such centres outside Ontario as may from time to time be authorised by the Senate. Applications for the establishment of such local centres must be made to the Registrar not later than the 15th of April in each year. Applications from candidates for this examination must be sent to the Registrar not later than the 1st of May.

A Junior Matriculation examination, at which no honour papers are set, will be held in September at the University and at such other centres as may from time to time be authorised by the Senate. Candidates who have failed in a minority of subjects at a previous examination, as well as new candidates, may present themselves at this examination. Applications must be sent to the Registrar not later than the 1st of September.

The presiding examiner's fee of $5.00 per diem, together with any other necessary expenses in connection with a local examination, must be met by the candidates at the centre, or by the authorities of the School or College on whose application it is held.

Candidates who have passed Junior Matriculation may present themselves at a subsequent examination for Junior Matriculation Scholarships. Such candidates will be exempt from the examinations in English Grammar and Arithmetic in 1906, but a person to whom a scholarship has been awarded may not compete a second time.

EQUIVALENT EXAMINATIONS.

A person who has passed the matriculation examination of another University may be admitted *ad eundem statum* on such conditions as the Senate, on application, may prescribe.

The local examinations conducted by the University of Oxford and Cambridge are accepted *pro tanto*.

Certificates of having passed the whole, or at least one-half, of the subjects of any of the following examinations will be accepted *pro tanto*.

Province of Ontario.

The Junior and Senior Leaving examinations, or examinations of the same standard under other names.

Candidates who have already passed Part I of the pass Junior Matriculation, or of the Junior Leaving examination, will not be required to pass again in the subjects thereof.

Province of Quebec.

The Associate in Arts examination.

Province of New Brunswick.

The examinations for Superior and Grammar School Licenses.

Province of Nova Scotia.

The Junior and Senior Leaving examinations.

Province of Manitoba.

The Second Class Teachers' Certificate.

Province of British Columbia.

The Intermediate and Senior Grade examination.

Province of Prince Edward Island.

The First Class Teachers' License examination.

North-West Territories.

The Standard VII. and VIII. examinations.

Newfoundland.

Intermediate and Associate Grade examinations.

Candidates whose certificates do not cover all the subjects may complete matriculation by passing in the remaining subjects as prescribed by the University, or by passing in the subjects of similar standard as prescribed by the Education Department of the Province by which the certificate was issued.

The Senate will consider applications for the recognition of certificates other than those mentioned, as occasion may require.

FEES.

The Fees payable are as follows:—

For Junior Matriculation.......................	$5 00
For supplemental examination in one subject......	2 00
For supplemental examination in two subjects....	4 00
For supplemental examination, maximum fee.....	5 00
For registration of certificates for other than University purposes...........................	5 00
For registration of certificates other than those of Ontario, which exempt the applicant from the full Matriculation examination..............	5 00
For admission *ad eundem statum*...............	5 00

JUNIOR MATRICULATION.

FOR PASS.

Greek.

Translation into English of passages from prescribed texts.

Translation at sight (with the aid of vocabularies) of easy Attic prose, to which special importance will be attached.

Grammatical questions on the passages from prescribed texts will be set, and such other questions as arise naturally from the context.

Translation from English into Greek of phrases and of sentences to illustrate Greek accidence and the common rules of Greek syntax.

The following are the prescribed texts:—

1907 and 1908: Xenophon, selections in White's First Greek Book, with the exercises thereon; Herodotus, Tales, ed. Farnell, I-XI., inclusive.

1909: Xenophon, selections in White's First Greek Book, with the exercises thereon; Herodotus, Tales, ed. Farnell, XI-XX., inclusive.

Two papers will be set: (1) Prescribed texts and questions on grammar; (2) the translation of English into Greek and sight translation.

Latin.

1907, 1908, 1909: Translation at sight of passages of average difficulty from Caesar, upon which special stress will be laid.

Translation from a prescribed portion of Virgil's Aeneid, with questions thereon.

Questions on Latin accidence.

Translation into Latin of English sentences to illustrate the common rules of Latin syntax, upon which special stress will be laid. The vocabulary will be taken from the prescribed portion of Caesar.

Examination upon a short prescribed portion of Caesar, to test the candidate's knowledge of Latin syntax and his power of idiomatic translation, etc.

The following are the texts prescribed:—

Caesar, Bellum Gallicum, Book IV., chaps. 20-38, and Book V., chaps. 1-23; Virgil, Aeneid, Book II., vv. 1-505.

Two papers will be set: (1) Translation at sight, Virgil, and accidence. (2) Translation into Latin, syntax, and idiomatic translation from prescribed Caesar, etc.

English.

GRAMMAR AND RHETORIC: The main facts in the development of the language. Etymology and syntax, including the logical structure of the sentence and the inflection, classification and elementary analysis of words. The rhetorical structure of the sentence and paragraph.

One examination paper.

COMPOSITION: An essay, to which special importance will be attached, on one of several themes set by the examiner.

One examination paper.

LITERATURE: The candidate will be expected to have memorised some of the finest passages. Besides questions to test the candidate's familiarity with, and comprehension of, the following selections, questions may also be set to determine within reasonable limits his power of appreciating literary art.

One examination paper.

1907: Tennyson, Ode to Memory, The Dying Swan, The Lotus Eaters, Ulysses, "You ask me, why," "Of old sat Freedom," "Love thou thy land," "Tears, idle tears," and the six interlude songs from the Princess, The Brook, Ode on the Duke of Wellington, Charge of the Light Brigade, Enoch Arden; Shakespeare, Julius Cæsar, Midsummer Night's Dream.

1908: Tennyson, The Poet, The Lady of Shalott, Oenone, The Epic and Morte d'Arthur, St. Agnes' Eve, The Voyage, "Break ,break, break," In the Valley of the Cauteretz; Browning, My Last Duchess, "How they brought the good news from Ghent to Aix," Love among the Ruins, Home Thoughts from Abroad, Up at a Villa, Andrea del Sarto, The Guardian Angel, Prospice, An Epistle of Karshish, Cavalier Tunes; Shakespeare, Macbeth, As You Like It.

1909: Coleridge, The Ancient Mariner; Wordsworth, Michael, Influence of Natural Objects, Nutting, Expostulation and Reply, The Tables Turned, The Solitary Reaper, Ode to Duty, Elegiac Stanzas, To the Rev. Dr. Wordsworth, "She was a phantom of delight," To the Cuckoo, The Green Linnet, "Bright flower! whose home," To a Skylark ("Ethereal minstrel! pilgrim of the sky!"), Reverie of Poor Susan, To my Sister, "Three years she grew," September, 1819, Upon the Same Occasion, and the following twelve sonnets:—"Two voices are there," "A flock of sheep that leisurely," "Earth hath not anything," "It is not to be thought of," "Fair star of evening," "O friend, I know not," "Milton, thou shouldst," "When I have borne in memory," "Brook! whose society," "Scorn not the sonnet," "Tax not the royal saint," "They dreamt not of a perishable home;" Shakespeare, Merchant of Venice, Henry V.

German.

The candidate's knowledge of German will be tested by: (1) simple questions on grammar; (2) the translation of simple passages from English into German; (3) translation at sight of easy passages from modern German, and (4) an examination on the following texts:—

Grimm, Rotkäppchen; Andersen, Wie's der Alte macht, Das neue Kleid, Venedig, Rothschild, Der Bär; Ertl, Himmelsschlüssel; Frommel, Das eiserne Kreuz; Baumbach, Nicotiana, Der Goldbaum; Heine, Lorelei, Du bist wie eine Blume; Uhland, Schäfer's Sonntagslied, Das

Schloss am Meer; Chamisso, Das Schloss Boncourt; Claudius, Die Sterne, Der Riese Goliath; Goethe, Mignon, Erlkönig, Der Sänger; Schiller, Der Jüngling am Bache.

1907: Hauff, Das Kalte Herz.

1908: Leander, Träumereien, pp. 45-90 (selected by Van Daell).

1909: Baumbach, Waldnovellen.

Two papers will be set: (1) Prescribed texts and translation at sight; questions on grammar; (2) the translation of English into German.

French.

The candidate's knowledge of French will be tested by: (1) simple questions on grammar; (2 the translation of simple passages from English into French; (3) translation at sight of easy passages from modern French, and (4) an examination on the following texts: —

Lamennais, Paroles d'un croyant, Chaps. VII. and XVII ; Perrault, le Maitre Chat ou le Chat Botté; Dumas, Un nez gelé, and la Pipe de Jean Bart; Alphonse Daudet, la Dernière classe, and la Chèvre de M. Seguin; Legouvé, la Patte de dindon; Pouvillon, Hortibus; Loti, Chagrin d'un vieux forçat; Molière, l'Avare, Acte III. sc. 5 (Est-ce à votre cocher . . . sous la mienne) ; Victor Hugo, Waterloo, Chap. IX.; Rouget de L'Isle, la Marseillaise; Arnault, la Feuille; Chateaubriand, l'Exilé; Théophile Gautier, la Chimère; Victor Hugo, Extase; Lamartine, l'Automne; De Musset, Tristesse; Sully Prudhomme, le Vase brisé; La Fontaine, le Chêne et le Roseau.

1907: Labiche, la Grammaire.

1908: Meilhac et Halévy, l'Eté de la Saint-Martin.

1909: Labiche, le Voyage de Monsieur Perrichon.

Two papers will be set: (1) Prescribed texts and translation at sight; questions on grammar; (2) the translation of English into French.

History.

Great Britain and Canada from 1763 to 1885, with the outlines of the preceding periods of British history.

The geography relating to the history prescribed.

One half examination paper.

General outlines of Greek history to the fall of Corinth.

General outlines of Roman history to the death of Augustus.

The geography relating to the history prescribed.

One half examination paper.

Mathematics.

ARITHMETIC.—Elementary Rules, Fractions (Vulgar and Decimal), Contracted Methods of Computation, Square Root, Interest, Discount, Commission, Insurance, Stocks and Exchange.

MENSURATION.—The Rectangle, the Parallelogram, the Triangle, the Circle, the Parallelopiped, the Prism, and the Cylinder.

One examination paper.

NOTE.—The problems proposed at this Examination will be simple and direct, and in their solution neatness and accuracy will be insisted on.

ALGEBRA: Elementary rules; highest common measure; lowest common multiple; fractions; square root; simple equations of one, two and three unknown quantities; indices; surds; quadratics of one and two unknown quantities.

One examination paper.

GEOMETRY: A.—CONSTRUCTIONS.

To construct a triangle with sides of given lengths.

To construct an angle equal to a given rectilineal angle.

To bisect a given angle.

To bisect a given straight line.

To draw a line perpendicular to a given line from a given point in it.

To draw a line perpendicular to a given line from a given point not in the line.

Locus of a point equidistant from two given lines.

Locus of a point equidistant from two given points.

To draw a line parallel to another, through a given point.

To divide a given line into any number of equal parts.

To describe a parallelogram equal to a given triangle, and having an angle equal to a given angle.

To describe a parallelogram equal to a given rectilineal figure, and having an angle equal to a given angle.

On a given straight line to describe a parallelogram equal to a given triangle, and having an angle equal to a given angle.

To find the centre of a given circle.

From a given point to draw a tangent to a given circle.

On a given straight line to construct a segment of a circle containing an angle equal to a given angle.

From a given circle to cut off a segment containing an angle equal to a given angle.

In a circle to inscribe a triangle equiangular to a given triangle.

To find locus of centres of circles touching two given lines.

To inscribe a circle in a given triangle.

To describe a circle touching three given straight lines.

To describe a circle about a given triangle.

About a given circle to describe a triangle equiangular to a given triangle.

To divide a given line similarly to another given divided line.

To find the fourth proportional to three given lines.

To describe a polygon similar to a given polygon, and with the corresponding sides in a given ratio.

To find the mean proportional between two given straight lines.

To construct a polygon similar to a given polygon, and such that their areas are in a given ratio.

To describe a polygon of a given shape and size.

B.—THEOREMS.

The sum of the angles of any triangle is equal to two right angles.

The angles at the base of an isosceles triangle are equal, with converse.

If the three sides of one triangle be equal, respectively, to the three sides of another, the triangles are equal in all respects.

If two sides and the included angle of one triangle be equal to two sides and the included angle of another triangle, the triangles are equal in all respects.

If two angles and one side of a triangle be equal to two angles and the corresponding side of another, the triangles are equal in all respects.

If two sides and an angle opposite one of these sides be equal, respectively, in two triangles, the angles opposite the other pair of equal sides are either equal or supplemental.

The sum of the exterior angles of a polygon is four right angles.

The greater side of any triangle has the greater angle opposite it.

The greater angle of any triangle has the greater side opposite it.

If two sides of one triangle be equal respectively to two sides of another, that with the greater contained angle has the greater base, with converse.

If a transversal fall on two parallel lines, relations between angles formed, with converse.

Lines which join equal and parallel lines towards the same parts are themselves equal and parallel.

The opposite sides and angles of a parallelogram are equal and the diagonal bisects it.

Parallelograms on the same base, or on equal bases, and between the same parallels are equal.

Triangles on the same base, or on equal bases, and between the same parallels are equal.

Triangles equal in area, and on the same base, are between the same parallels.

If a parallelogram and a triangle be on the same base, and between the same parallels, the parallelogram is double the triangle.

Expressions for area of a parallelogram, and area of a triangle.

The complements of the parallelogram about the diagonal of any parallelogram are equal.

The square on the hypotenuse of a right-angled triangle is equal to the sum of the squares on the sides.

If a straight line be divided into any two parts, the sum of the squares on the parts, together with twice the rectangle contained by the parts, is equal to the square on the whole line.

The square on a side of any triangle is equal to the sum of the squares on the two other sides + twice the rectangle contained by either of these sides and the projection of the other side on it.

If more than two equal straight lines can be drawn from the circumference of a circle to a point within it, that point is the centre.

The diameter is the greatest chord in a circle, and a chord nearer the centre is greater than one more remote. Also the greater chord is nearer the centre than the less.

The angle at the centre of a circle is double the angle at the circumference on the same arc.

The angles in the same segment of a circle are equal, with converse.

The opposite angles of a quadrilateral inscribed in a circle are together equal to two right angles, with converse.

The angle in a semicircle is a right angle; in a segment greater than a semicircle less than a right angle, in a segment less than a semicircle greater than a right angle.

A tangent is perpendicular to the radius to the point of contact; only one tangent can be drawn at a given point; the perpendicular to the tangent at the point of contact passes through the centre; the perpendicular from centre on tangent passes through the point of contact.

If two circles touch, the line joining the centres passes through the point of contact.

The angles which a chord drawn from the point of contact makes with the tangent, are equal to the angles in the alternate segments.

The rectangles under the segments of intersecting chords are equal.

If $OA.OB.=OC^2$, OC is a tangent to the circle through A, B and C.

Triangles of the same altitude are as their bases.

A line parallel to the base of a triangle divides the sides proportionally, with converse.

If a vertical angle of a triangle be bisected, the bisector divides the base into segments that are as the sides, with converse.

The analogous proposition when the exterior angle at the vertex is bisected, with converse.

If two triangles are equiangular, the sides are proportional.

If the sides of two triangles are proportional, the triangles are equiangular.

If the sides of two triangles about equal angles are proportional, the triangles are equiangular.

If two triangles have an angle in each equal, and the sides about two other angles proportional, the remaining angles are equal or supplemental.

Similar triangles are as the squares on corresponding sides.

The perpendicular from the right angle of a right-angled triangle on the hypotenuse divides the triangle into two which are similar to the original triangle.

In equal circles angles, whether at the centres or circumferences, are proportional to the arcs on which they stand.

The areas of two similar polygons are as the squares on corresponding sides.

If three lines be proportional, the first is to the third as the figure on the first to a similar figure on the second.

Questions and easy deductions on the preceding constructions and theorems.

It is recommended that the study of formal demonstrative Geometry be preceded by a course in Practical Geometry, extending over not more than a year, and embracing the following:—

Definitions; fundamental geometric conceptions and principles; use of simple instruments, as compasses, protractor, graduated rule, etc.; measurement of lines and angles, and construction of lines and angles of given numerical magnitude; accurate construction of figures; some leading propositions in plane geometry reached by induction as a result of accurate construction of figures; deduction also employed as principles are reached and assured. At the examination questions may be given in Practical Geometry, the constructions being such as naturally spring from the prescribed course. Candidates must provide themselves with a graduated ruler, compasses, set-square and protractor.

In the formal deductive Geometry modifications of Euclid's treatment of the subject will be allowed, though not required, as follows:—

The employment of the "hypothetical construction."

The free employment of the method of superposition, including the rotation of figures about an axis, or about a point in a plane.

A modification of Euclid's parallel postulate.

A treatment of ratio and proportion restricted to the case in which the compared magnitudes are commensurable.

One examination paper.

Elementary Experimental Science.

PHYSICS: Use of meter rule; use of calipers and vernier for more accurate metric measurements (e.g., diameters of wires, thickness of glass, plates, etc.); numerical calculations in the metric system.

Use of balance.

Specific gravity, by special gravity bottle and hydrostatic balance, of liquids and of solids.

Boyle's law; barometer; diffusion of gases.

Use of Fahrenheit and centigrade thermometers; determination of zero and boiling point; boiling point dependent on pressure.

Expansion of solids, liquids and gases; examples.

Specific heat, latent heat; easy numerical examples.

Transmutation of matter; indestructibility of matter.

Solution, precipitation, crystallisation and evaporation.

One half examination paper.

CHEMISTRY: Properties of hydrogen, chlorine, oxygen, sulphur, nitrogen, carbon, and their different compounds, especially those of economic and industrial importance.

Mixtures, solutions, chemical compounds, elements, nomenclature, laws of chemical combinations, e.g., combining weights, chemical formulæ and equations, with easy numerical examples.

One half examination paper.

FOR HONOURS.

Greek.

Translation into English of passages from prescribed texts.

Translation at sight of prose passages of average difficulty, similar to the authors read.

Grammatical questions on the passages from prescribed texts will be set, and such other questions as arise naturally from the context.

Translation into Greek of ordinary narrative passages of English, similar in style to the authors read.

The following are the prescribed texts:—

1907: Xenophon, Selections in White's First Greek Book; Herodotus, Tales, ed. Farnell I.-XI. incl.; Homer, Odyssey XXI.; Lucian, Timon; Lysias, Pro Mantitheo and de Invalido.

1908: Xenophon, Selections in White's First Greek Book; Herodotus, Tales, ed. Farnell I.-XI. incl.; Homer, Odyssey, XXIII.; Lucian, Timon; Lysias, Pro Mantitheo and de Invalido.

1909: Xenophon, Selections in White's First Greek Book; Herodotus, Tales, ed. Farnell XL-XX. incl.; Homer, Odyssey XXIII.; Lucian, Charon; Lysias, Contra Eratosthenem.

Two examination papers.

Latin.

Translation into English of passages from prescribed texts.

Translation at sight of passages of average difficulty from Cicero.

Grammatical questions on the passages from prescribed texts will be set, and such other questions as arise naturally from the context.

Translation into Latin of easy passages of English, similar in style to the authors read.

The following are the prescribed texts:—

1907: Caesar, Bellum Gallicum, Book IV., Chaps. 20-38, and Book V., Chaps. 1-23; Virgil, Aeneid, Book II.; Horace, Odes, Books III. and IV.; Cicero, Pro Lege Manilia, Pro Marcello.

1908: Caesar, Bellum Gallicum, Book IV., Chaps. 20-38, and Book V., Chaps. 1-23; Virgil, Aeneid, Book IL; Horace, Odes, Books III., IV., Cicero, In Catilinam I., III., IV.

1909: Caesar, Bellum Gallicum, Book IV., Chaps. 20-38 and Book V., Chaps. 1-23; Virgil, Aeneid, Book II.; Horace, Odes, Books I., II.; Cicero, In Catilinam I., III., IV.

Two examination papers: (1) Latin Prose, (2) Authors and Sight.

English.

COMPOSITION: An essay on one of several themes set by the examiners. In order to pass in this subject, legible writing, correct spelling and punctuation, and proper construction of sentences are indispensable. The candidate should also give attention to the structure of the whole essay, the effective ordering of the thought, and the accurate employment of a good English vocabulary. About two pages of foolscap is suggested as the proper length for the essay; but quality, not quantity, will be mainly regarded.

One examination paper.

LITERATURE: Such questions only will be set as may serve to test the candidate's familiarity with, and intelligent and appreciative comprehension of, the prescribed texts. The candidate will be expected to have memorised some of the finest passages. In addition to the questions on the prescribed selections others will be set on a "sight passage" to test the candidate's ability to interpret literature for himself.

One examination paper.

1907: Tennyson, Ode to Memory, The Dying Swan, The Lotus Eaters, Ulysses, "You ask me, why," "Of old sat Freedom," "Love thou thy land," "Tears, idle tears," and the six interlude songs from The Princess, The Brook, Ode on the Duke of Wellington, Charge of the Light Brigade, Enoch Arden; Shakespeare, Julius Caesar.

1908: Tennyson, The Poet, The Lady of Shalott, ´ ᴕᴨ ne, The Epic and Morte d'Arthur, St. Agnes' Eve, The Voyage, "Break, .reak, break," In the Valley of the Cauteretz; Browning, My Last Duchess, "How they brought the good news from Ghent to Aix," Love among the Ruins, Home Thoughts from Abroad, Up at a Villa, Andrea del Sarto, The Guardian Angel, Prospice, An Epistle of Karshish, Cavalier Tunes, Shakespeare, Macbeth.

1909: Coleridge, The Ancient Mariner; Wordsworth, Michael, Influence of Natural Objects, Nutting, Expostulations and Reply, The Tables Turned, The Solitary Reaper, Ode to Duty, Elegiac Stanzas, To the Rev. Dr. Wordsworth, "She was a phantom of delight," To the Cuckoo, The Green Linnet, "Bright flower! whose home," To a Skylark, ("Ethereal minstrel! pilgrim of the sky!"), Reverie of Poor Susan, To my Sister, "Three years she grew in sun and shade," September 1819, Upon the same Occasion. The following twelve sonnets: "Two voices are there," "Scorn not the sonnet." "A flock of sheep that leisurely," "Earth hath not anything," "It is not to be thought of," "Fair star of evening," "O friend! I know not," "Milton! thou shouldst," "When I have borne in memory," "Brook! whose society," "Tax not the royal saint," "They dreamt not of a perishable home;" Shakespeare, Merchant of Venice.

German.

The prescription of work in grammar, the translation of English into German and sight translation is the same for honours as for pass, but the examination will be of a more advanced character.

The following are the prescribed texts:—

Grimm, Rotkäppchen; Andersen, Wie's der Alte macht, Das neue Kleid, Venedig, Rothschild, Der Bär; Ertl, Himmelsschlüssel; Frommel, Das eiserne Kreuz; Baumbach, Nicotiana, Der Goldbaum; Heine, Lorelei, Du bist wie eine Blume; Uhland, Schäfer's Sonntagslied, Das Schloss am Meer; Chamisso, Das Schloss Boncourt; Claudius, Die Sterne, Der Riese Goliath; Goethe, Mignon, Erlkönig, Der·Sänger; Schiller, Der Jüngling am Bache.

1907: Hauff, Das kalte Herz.

Baumbach, Der Schwiegersohn; Elz, Er ist nicht eifersüchtig; Wichert, Post Festum.

1908: Leander, Träumereien, pp. 45 to 90⁻ (selected by Van Daell).

Baumbach, Der Schwiegersohn; Elz, Er ist nicht eifersüchtig; Wichert, Post Festum.

1909: Baumbach, Waldnovellen; Zschokke, Der tote Gast.

French.

The prescription of work in grammar, the translation of English into French and sight translation, is the same for honours as for pass, but the examination will be of a more advanced character.

The following are the prescribed texts:—

Lamennais, Paroles d'un croyant, Chaps. VII. and XVII.; Perrault, le Maître Chat ou le Chat botté; Dumas, Un nez gelé, and la Pipe de Jean Bart; Alphonse Daudet, la Dernière Classe, and la Chèvre de M. Seguin; Legouvé, la Patte de dindon; Pouvillon, Hortibus; Loti, Chagrin d'un vieux forçat; Molière, l'Avare, Acte III., sc. 5 (Est-ce à votre cocher . . . sous la mienne); Victor Hugo, Waterloo, Chap. IX.; Rouget de l'Isle, la Marseillaise; Arnault, la Feuille; Chateaubriand, l'Exilé; Théophile Gautier, la Chimère; Victor Hugo, Extase; Lamartine, l'Automne; De Musset, Tristesse; Sully Prudhomme, le Vase brisé; La Fontaine, le Chêne et le Roseau.

1907: Labiche, la Grammaire; Sand, la Mare au Diable.

1908: Meilhac et Halévy, l'Eté de la Saint-Martin; Chateaubriand, Mémoires d'Outre-Tombe (selections pub. by Clarendon Press).

1909: Labiche, le Voyage de Monsieur Perrichon; Mérimée, Quatre Contes, ed. by F. C. L. Steenderen (Holt & Co.).

History.

English history from the discovery of America to 1763.
General outlines of Greek history to the fall of Corinth.
General outlines of Roman history to the death of Augustus.
The geography relating to the history prescribed.
One examination paper.

Mathematics.

ALGEBRA: Elementary rules; highest common measure; lowest common multiple; fractions; square root; simple equations of one, two and three unknown quantities; indices; surds, quadratics of one and two unknown quantities; theory of divisors; ratio, proportion and variation; progressions; notation; permutations and combinations; binomial theorem; interest forms; annuities.
One examination paper.

TRIGONOMETRY: Trigonometrical ratios with their relations to each other; sines, etc., of the sum and difference of angles with deduced formulas; use of logarithms; solution of triangles; expressions for the area of triangles; radii of circumscribed, inscribed and escribed circles.
One examination paper.

PROBLEMS: One paper.

GEOMETRY: A.—Exercises on the course prescribed for the Pass Examination, with special reference to the following topics—Loci; Maxima and Minima; The System of Inscribed, Escribed and Circumscribed Circles of a Triangle, with metrical relations; Radical Axis.

B.—The following additional propositions in Synthetic Geometry, with exercises thereon:—

To divide a given straight line internally and externally in medial section.

To describe a square that shall be equal to a given rectilineal figure.

To describe an isosceles triangle having each of the angles at the base double of the third angle.

To inscribe a regular pentagon in a given circle.

The squares on two sides of a triangle are together equal to twice the square on half the third side and twice the square on the median to that side.

If A B C be a triangle, and A be joined to a point P of the base such that $B P : P C = m : n$, then $n \, A \, B^2 + m \, A \, C^2 = (m + n) \, A \, P^2 + n \, B \, P^2 + m \, P \, C^2$.

In a right-angled triangle the rectilineal figure described on the hypotenuse is equal to the sum of the similar and similarly described figures on the two other sides.

If the vertical angle of a triangle be bisected by a straight line which also cuts the base, the rectangle contained by the sides of the triangle is equal to the rectangle contained by the segments of the base, together with the square on the straight line which bisects the angle.

If from the vertical angle of a triangle a straight line be drawn perpendicular to the base, the rectangle contained by the sides of the triangle is equal to the rectangle contained by the perpendicular and the diameter of the circle described about the triangle.

The rectangle contained by the diagonals of a quadrilateral inscribed in a circle is equal to the sum of the two rectangles contained by its opposite sides.

Two similar polygons may be so placed that the lines joining corresponding points are concurrent.

If a straight line meet the sides B C, C A, A B, of a triangle A B C in D, E, F, respectively, then B' D. C E. A F = D C. E A. F B, and conversely. (Menelaus' Theorem.)

If straight lines through the angular points A, B, C of a triangle are concurrent, and intersect the opposite sides in D, E, F, respectively, then B' D. C E. A F = D C. E A. F B and conversely. (Ceva's Theorem.)

If a point A lie on the polar of a point B with respect to a circle, then B lies on polar of A.

Any straight line which passes through a fixed point is cut harmonically by the point, any circle, and the polar of the point with respect to the circle.

In a complete quadrilateral each diagonal is divided harmonically by the two other diagonals, and the angular points through which it passes.

C.—Elementary Analytical Geometry: Axes of co-ordinates. Position of a point in plane of reference.

Transformation of co-ordinates,—origin changed, or axes (rectangular) turned through a given angle.

$$\pm 2\, A = x_1\, (y_2 - y_3) + \ldots + \ldots$$

Co-ordinates of point dividing line joining $P_1\, (x_1, y_1)$ and $P_2\, (x_2, y_2)$ in ratio $m : n$ are

$$x = \frac{m\, x_2 + n\, x_1}{m + n}, \quad y = \frac{m\, y_2 + n\, y_1}{m + n}.$$

$$(P_1\, P_2)^2 = (x_1 - x_2)^2 + (y_1 - y_2)^2$$

Equations of straight lines.

$$\left. \begin{array}{l} \dfrac{x - x_1}{x_1 - x_2} = \dfrac{y - y_1}{y_1 - y_2} \\[2mm] \dfrac{x}{a} + \dfrac{y}{b} = 1. \end{array} \right\} \quad \begin{array}{l} \text{Line defined by two points} \\ \text{through which it passes.} \end{array}$$

$$\left.\begin{aligned} &\frac{x-a}{\cos\theta}=\frac{y-b}{\sin\theta}=r. \\ &y=mx+b. \\ &y=m(x-a). \\ &x\cos\alpha+y\sin\alpha=p. \end{aligned}\right\}$$ Line defined by one point through which it passes, and by its direction.

General equation of 1st degree, $Ax+By+C=0$, represents a straight line.

Any line through (x_1, y_1) is
$$A(x-x_1)+B(y-y_1)=0.$$

If θ be angle between $Ax+By+C=0$ and $A'x+B'y+C'=0$, then
$$\tan\theta=\frac{A'B-AB'}{AA'+BB'}$$

Condition of $\perp$ rity, $AA'+BB'=0$.

Condition of ‖ ism, $\dfrac{A}{A'}=\dfrac{B}{B'}$.

Distance from (a, b) to $Ax+By+C=0$, in direction whose direction cosines are (l, m) is
$$\frac{Aa+Bb+C}{Al+Bm}.$$

$\perp$ distance from (a, b) on $Ax+By+C=0$.
$$=\frac{Aa+Bb+C}{\sqrt{A^2+B^2}}.$$

THE CIRCLE—

Equations in forms :
$$x^2+y^2=r^2.$$
$$(x-a)^2+(y-b)^2=r^2.$$
$$y^2=2rx-x^2.$$

General equation $x^2+y^2+2Ax+2By+C=0$,
or $(x+A)^2+(y+B)^2=A^2+B^2-C$,
represents a circle with centre $(-A, -B)$ and radius
$$\sqrt{A^2+B^2-C}.$$

Tangent at (x', y') to $x^2+y^2=r^2$, is $xx'+yy'=r^2$.

Normal is $\dfrac{x}{x'}=\dfrac{y}{y'}$.

Tangent in form
$$y=mx\pm r\sqrt{1+m^2}.$$

Pole being (x', y'), polar is $xx'+yy'=r^2$.

If pole move along a line, polar turns about pole of that line.

Square of length of tangent from
$$(x', y') \text{ to } x^2+y^2+2Ax+2By+C=0$$
is $x'^2+y'^2+2Ax'+2By'+C$.

Radical axis of
$$x^2+y^2+2Ax+2By+C=0,$$
$$x^2+y^2+2A'x+2B'y+C'=0.$$

Easy exercises on the preceding propositions.

Physics.

MECHANICS: Measurement of velocity; uniformly accelerated rectilineal motion; metre; units of force, work, energy and power; equilibrium of forces acting at a point; triangle, parallelogram, and polygon of forces; parallel forces; principle of moments; centre of gravity; laws of friction; numerical examples.

HYDROSTATICS: Fluid pressure at a point; pressure on a horizontal plane; pressure on an inclined plane; resultant vertical pressure, and resultant horizontal pressure, when fluid is under air pressure and when not; transmission of pressure; Bramah's press; equilibrium of liquids of unequal density in a bent tube; the barometer; air-pump; water-pump, common and force; siphon.

ELECTRICITY: Voltaic cells, common kinds; chemical action in the cell; magnetic effects of the current; chemical effects of the current; voltameters; electroplating; astatic and tangent galvanometers; simple notions of potential; Ohm's law; shunts; measurement of resistance; electric light, arc and incandescent; current induction; induction coil; dynamo and motor; the joule and watt; electric bell; telegraph; telephone; elements of terrestrial magnetism.

One examination paper.

Chemistry.

Chemical and physical reactions, rates of reactions, reversible reactions, chemical equilibrium. The practical study of the following elements with their most characteristic compounds, having regard to Mendelejeff's classification of the elements, and some of the most important economic and industrial applications: hydrogen, sodium, potassium, magnesium, zinc, calcium, strontium, barium, boron, aluminium, carbon, silicon, tin lead, nitrogen, phosphorus, arsenic, antimony, bismuth, oxygen, sulphur, fluorine, chlorine, bromine, iodine, manganese, iron, copper, nickel. A report must be furnished showing the amount and nature of the laboratory work done by each candidate, and the teacher's opinion of his proficiency.

One examination paper.

Biology.

1. ELEMENTS OF ZOOLOGY: The candidate will be examined practically on his acquaintance with the structure of the various types prescribed below, and must be prepared to sketch the specimens submitted to him.

Vertebrate Types: 1. The fish:—Any one of the common fresh water fishes of Ontario may be employed for the purpose; special attention should be given to the organs of locomotion, circulation, respiration. As several species are easily obtainable this class may be employed for studying the principles of zoological nomenclature.

2. The frog:—Comparison with the fish as to the organs above mentioned—observation of the development of the spawn of one or more Amphibia.

3. The reptile:—A study of the external form of a turtle and a snake, and cómparison of both with a lizard.

4. The bird:—Special attention should be given to the plumage, the bill and feet, and to the modifications of the skeletal, muscular and respiratory systems in connection with aerial life.

5. The mammal:—Characters of the chief domesticated and wild mammals of Ontario must be studied, as well as the main facts of internal structure of one of the smaller forms (the rabbit, e.g.). Comparison of the teeth and feet of the pig, horse, sheep, rabbit, dog, mole, bat.

Invertebrate Types: 1. Study of the Crayfish as a type of the arthropods. Comparison of the external form of the Crayfish with an insect (*e.g.*, grasshopper, cricket or cockroach) also with a millipede and a spider.

2. Unsegmented and segmented worms.

3. Fresh water mussel and snail.

4. A fresh water unicellular animal such as an Amoeba or Paramecium.

The natural habits of the various animals studied.

Elements of zoological classification based on forms studied.

2. ELEMENTS OF BOTANY: The examination will test whether the candidate has practically studied representatives of the flowering plants of the locality in which the preparatory school is situated, and representative plants.

REGULATIONS RELATING TO DEGREES IN MEDICINE.

The Degrees in Medicine are Bachelor of Medicine (M.B.), and Doctor of Medicine (M.D.).

BACHELOR OF MEDICINE.

Candidates for the degree of Bachelor of Medicine are required to matriculate and to attend during four sessions of at least eight months each the courses of instruction presented, and to pass four examinations taken in the following order: the First at the end of the first session; the Second at the end of the second session; the Third at the end of the third session; and the Fourth at the end of the fourth session.

ENTRANCE.

Candidates for a degree must pass the Matriculation examination, unless (1) they possess a degree in Arts not being an Honorary Degree, from any Dominion or British University; or (2) have already matriculated in the Faculty of Arts or in the Faculty of Law in this University; or (3) have been registered as Matriculates in the College of Physicians and Surgeons of Ontario.

Students who have not completed matriculation may be admitted to the courses of instruction of the Second Year, but not to the examination of that year.

No fee will be charged for transferring from the Faculty of Arts to that of Medicine.

REGISTRATION.

Students entering the University are required to submit the certificates on which they claim standing to the Registrar not later than the first day of November.

Candidates who at the close of the Supplemental examinations have failed to secure standing will not be eligible for registration in the next higher year.

ATTENDANCE.

Candidates are required to attend lectures and receive practical instruction during each of four years at this University.

The Senate may accept certificates of attendance at the lectures and practical instruction in the laboratories of affiliated and other recognized institutions.

EXAMINATIONS.

The annual examinations are styled the First, Second, Third, Fourth and Fifth examinations, and are to be passed at the end of the First, Second, Third, Fourth and Fifth academic years respectively.

The annual examinations are held in May, and the supplemental examinations in September.

Candidates at any examination who have passed in the majority of the subjects required may present themselves at the supplemental examinations next ensuing, in the subjects in which they failed, and on passing at such examinations, shall be allowed their year.

Undergraduates below the standing of the Fourth Year, who have been rejected or who have been prevented from attending the annual examinations, by sickness, domestic affliction, or other causes beyond their control, may present themselves for examination at the Supplemental examinations in September.

Candidates who failed to attend at the annual examinations must prove to the satisfaction of the Vice-Chancellor before presenting themselves in September, the existence and sufficiency of the alleged cause of absence.

Undergraduates of the Fourth Year who have failed in not more than three subjects may present themselves for examination in the said subjects at the Supplemental examinations in September.

Graduates of this University in the Honour Department of Biological and Physical Sciences may enter at the beginning of the Third Year and may postpone the examination in Materia Medica and Elementary Therapeutics until the Third examination.

In the case of Graduates or Undergraduates in Natural Sciences or Biology, certificates of attendance on the second course of Practical Anatomy and on the second course of fifty lectures on Anatomy, may be presented with the certificates of attendance on the lectures of the Third Year.

Every undergraduate who proposes to present himself at an examination must send to the Registrar a statement (according to a printed form which will be furnished) of the course he is taking, whether he intends to compete for Honours, and such other particulars as the printed form may indicate, together with the original certificates referred to in this statement.

The work in the laboratories and in the wards of the hospitals during the session is an essential part of the instruction and will be considered in determining standing at any examination.

Before admission to examination the candidate is required to submit evidence of having complied with the regulations respecting attendance laboratory and clinical work in each of the subjects of instruction for the year in which he seeks examination. A certificate is issued by the

University, and must be signed by the head or heads of each department of instruction.

The following Honour courses of instruction and examinations in the
Faculty of Arts are accepted in the place of courses of instruction and
examinations in the Faculty of Medicine, according to the subjoined
scheme:—

Faculty of Arts.		Faculty of Medicine.
1. First Year Biology.	equivalent to	First Year Biology.
2. First Year Physics.	equivalent to	First Year Physics (with the exception of the Sound, Light and Electricity of this course).
3. First Year Chemistry.	equivalent to	First Year Chemistry.
4. Second Year Chemistry of the Honour course in Biology.	equivalent to	Second Year Chemistry.
5. Physiology and Physiological Chemistry of the Third and Fourth Years of the Honour courses in Biology and Biological and Physical Sciences.	equivalent to	First and Second Year Physiology and Physiological Chemistry.
6. Cytology and Histology of Third Year of Honour course of Biology and Biological and Physical Sciences.	equivalent to	Histology of Second Year.
7. Embryology of Fourth Year in Biology and Biological and Physical Sciences.	equivalent to	Embryology of Second Year.
8. Anatomy of Third and Fourth Years of the Honour course in Biological and Physical Sciences.	equivalent to	Anatomy of First and Second Years.

EQUIVALENT EXAMINATIONS.

Courses of lectures and examinations in the Faculty of Arts are accepted in the place of courses of lectures and examinations in the Faculty of Medicine, according to the following scheme:—

Faculty of Arts.		Faculty of Medicine.
1. Honour course and examination in Second Year Biology.	equivalent to	course and examination in First Year Biology, and course in First Year Physiology.
2. Honour course and examination in Second Year Chemistry, and Physics of the Honour course in Natural Sciences or Biological and Physical Sciences.	equivalent to	course and examination in First Year Inorganic Chemistry and Physics.
3. Honour course and examination in Third Year Chemistry.	equivalent to	course and examination in Second Year Chemistry (with the exception of Chemistry applied to Physiology).
4. Honour course and examination in Fourth Year Biology.	equivalent to	course and examination in Second Year Physiology and Embryology and Histology.

5. Attendance at the Honour course and examination in the Fourth Year Physiological Chemistry, in the Faculty of Arts, is equivalent to attendance at the course and examination in Chemistry applied to Physiology of the Second Year in the Faculty of Medicine.

Candidates who desire to compete for scholarships and medals are required to submit to the annual examinations in all the subjects of each examination, though otherwise entitled to partial exemption according to the preceding scheme; and candidates not competing for scholarships or medals, who are entitled to exemption according to the preceding scheme, will rank in Honours in these subjects.

COURSES OF INSTRUCTION.

A full course extends over a period of eight months.

First Year.

COURSES OF EIGHT MONTHS EACH—

1. Anatomy.
2. Practical Anatomy.

3. Biology.
4. Practical Biology.
5. Physiology.
6. Practical Physiology.
7. Inorganic Chemistry.
8. Practical Chemistry.

COURSES OF FOUR MONTHS EACH—

1. Physics.
2. Practical Physics.

Second Year.

COURSES OF EIGHT MONTHS EACH—

1. Anatomy.
2. Practical Anatomy.
3. Physiology.
4. Practical Physiology.
5. Embryology and Histology.
6. Methods of Physical Examination.

COURSES OF FOUR MONTHS EACH—

1. Organic Chemistry.
2. Practical Chemistry.
3. Practical Physiological Chemistry.
4. Pharmacy.
5. Pharmacology.

Third Year.

COURSES OF EIGHT MONTHS EACH—

1. Medicine.
2. Clinical Medicine.
3. Surgery.
4. Clinical Surgery.
5. Pathology.
6. Practical Pathology.
7. Obstetrics.
8. Attendance in the wards of a general hospital having not less than 100 beds.

COURSES OF FOUR MONTHS EACH—

1. Therapeutics.
2. Jurisprudence and Toxicology.
3. Topographical Anatomy.

A COURSE OF TWO MONTHS—

Clinical instruction in contagious diseases and vaccination.

Fourth Year.

COURSES OF EIGHT MONTHS EACH—

1. Medicine.
2. Clinical Medicine.
3. Surgery.
4. Clinical Surgery.
5. Pathology.
6. Practical Pathology.
7. Obstetrics.
8. Ophthalmology (examination of the eye, commoner diseases); Otology (examination of the ear, commoner diseases); Rhinology and ·Laryngology (commoner diseases of the nose and throat).
9. Attendance in the wards of a general hospital having not less than 100 beds.

COURSES OF FOUR MONTHS EACH—

1. Gynæcology.
2. Hygiene and Preventive Medicine.

COURSES OF TWO MONTHS EACH—

1. Mental Diseases.
2. Regional Anatomy.

At the Fourth examination, the candidate is required to submit the following certificates:—

1. Of having conducted at least six labours.
2. Of proficiency in vaccination.
   Of having attended twelve autopsies.

The certificate of a registered practitioner will be accepted in respect of 1 and 2.

Fifth Year.

COURSES OF SIX MONTHS EACH—

1. Medicine.
2. Clinical Medicine.
3. Surgery.
4. Clinical Surgery.
5. Pathology (gross and microscopical).
6. Clinical Gynæcology and Operative Obstetrics.
7. Ophthalmology, Otology, Laryngology and Rhinology.

COURSES OF THREE MONTHS EACH—

1. Special Therapeutics.
2. Regional Anatomy.
3. Advanced Physiology of the digestive and nervous systems.

A COURSE OF AT LEAST TWO MONTHS—

Anæsthetics.

1. History of Medicine.
2. Life Assurance.

The lectures in the Fifth year are not to exceed two per diem, the remainder of the day is to be devoted to laboratory and hospital work.

SUBJECTS OF THE DIFFERENT EXAMINATIONS.

FIRST EXAMINATION.

1. Physics.
2. Chemistry (Inorganic).
3. Biology.

SECOND EXAMINATION.

1. Anatomy.
2. Physiology.
3. Embryology and Histology.
4. Materia Medica and Elementary Therapeutics.
5. Chemistry (Organic and Physiological).
6. Methods of Physical Examination.

THIRD EXAMINATION.

1. Medicine and Clinical Medicine.
2. Surgery and Clinical Surgery.
3. Pathology.
4. Obstetrics.
5. Therapeutics.
6. Jurisprudence and Toxicology.
7. Topographical Anatomy.

The results of this examination will be considered in determining standing at the Fourth examination.

FOURTH EXAMINATION.

1. Medicine and Clinical Medicine.
2. Surgery and Clinical Surgery.
3. Pathology.
4. Obstetrics.
5. Ophthalmology, Otology, Rhinology and Laryngology.
6. Gynæcology.
7. Hygiene and Preventive Medicine.
8. Mental Diseases.
9. Regional Anatomy.

FIFTH EXAMINATION.

1. Medicine and Clinical Medicine.
2. Surgery and Clinical Surgery.

3. Pathology.
4. Gynæcology.
5. Obstetrics.
6. Ophthalmology, Otology, Laryngology and Rhinology.
7. Special Therapeutics.
8. Regional Anatomy.
9. Advanced Physiology.
10. Anæsthetics.
11. History of Medicine.
12. Life Assurance.

EXAMINATIONS FOR HONOURS.

Candidates taking seventy-five per cent. of the aggregate number of marks in the Pass and Honour Papers of the First or Second examination, or of one or more of the groups of subjects in the First examination will be placed in the Honour list.

Additional papers on all Pass subjects of an examination may be set for the Honour candidates.

The subjects of the Final examination are grouped for Honours as follows:—

Group   I. 1. Medicine and Clinical Medicine.
         2. Pathology.
         3. Therapeutics.

Group   II. 1. Surgery and Clinical Surgery.
         2. Pathology.
         3. Topographical Anatomy.

Group III. 1. Obstetrics.
         2. Gynæcology.
         3. Pathology.

Group IV. 1. Medical Jurisprudence and Toxicology.
         2. Hygiene.
         3. Medical Psychology.

Only those candidates will receive their degree with Honours who have obtained Honours in the First, Second and Final examinations.

ADMISSION AD EUNDEM STATUM.

Undergraduates of other Universities applying for admission *ad eundem statum* must present certificates of having passed the examinations in the various subjects of this curriculum preliminary to the examination for which they desire to present themselves.

DEGREE OF M. D.

Bachelors of Medicine of at least one year's standing may obtain the degree of M.D. on the fulfilment of either of the following conditions:—

1. Having presented an approved thesis embodying the results of an original research conducted by the candidate in any department of medicine; or

2. Having passed the fifth examination.

ADMISSION AD EUNDEM GRADUM.

A graduate of any of the Universities in Great Britain or Ireland, if his degree be not an honorary one, may be admitted to the like degree in the University of Toronto. He must send in his certificate to the Registrar at least two weeks before the first meeting of the session of the Senate of which his application is to be brought forward.

MEDALS AND SCHOLARSHIPS.

Medals.

The Faculty offers a gold medal and three silver medals annually for competition among those students of the Medical Faculty who are Honour candidates for the degree of M.B., which will be awarded by the Senate on the recommendation of the examiners.

Undergraduate Scholarships.

The following scholarships are annually offered for competition amongst students who attend the Lectures of the University Medical Faculty:—

At First Examination.............................one of $50
At First Examination.............................one of $30
At Second Examination.............................one of $50
At Second Examination.............................one of $30

Every student taking a scholarship is required to sign a declaration that it is his intention to pursue his medical studies for two or three years, according to the year in which he has taken such scholarship, and to proceed to a degree in the University of Toronto, and that he is not an undergraduate or graduate in the Faculty of Medicine of any other University.

No scholarship will be awarded to any candidate who has not obtained honours in the examination for which it is conferred.

Each scholarship is tenable for one year only, but a scholar of one year is eligible for the scholarship of a succeeding year.

The scholarships or medals are not open to those who are at the same time undergraduates or graduates in Medicine of another University.

No undergraduate in the Honour course, who shall have degraded into a lower year, shall be permitted at any ensuing examination to compete for medals or scholarships, except by special permission of the Faculty, to be granted only in case of illness or for other grave reasons,

THE GEORGE BROWN MEMORIAL SCHOLARSHIP IN MEDICAL SCIENCE.

Dr. A. H. F. Barbour, of Edinburgh, having placed a sum of money at the disposal of the University of Toronto, for the purpose of found-ing a Scholarship in Medical Science in memory of the late Hon. George Brown, the following regulations have been adopted with regard thereto:

This scholarship shall be called the George Brown Memorial Scholar-ship in Medical Science and shall be awarded annually at the Convoca-tion for conferring degrees in Medicine to the Bachelor of Medicine who shall have distinguished himself most during the Undergraduate course in the Honour course in Biological and Physical Science.

The award shall be made by a committee composed of the Profes-sors in these subjects, who shall report as to the successful candidates, after having given due attention to the results of the annual examina-tions, and to the character of the work done by the candidates in the University laboratories.

The holder of the scholarship during the year of tenure is required to engage in original research in any one of the laboratories of the Uni-versity, on some subject bearing on the advancement of medical science —the laboratory providing the material for the investigation.

The scholarship is to be paid in two portions, two-thirds at the time of award and one-third six months later, on the holder giving a satis-factory report (to whomsoever the University may appoint) of the work he has already done.

A report of the research, when completed, is to be given to the Uni-versity.

The value of the scholarship consists in the proceeds of one thousand pounds sterling, invested at the rate of interest secured by the Univer-sity for such benefactions.

The Reeve Scholarship.

The Reeve Post-graduate Scholarship, amounting to $250, which had been given for four years by the Dean of the Faculty, has, through the generosity of P. C. Larkin, Esq., been continued and will be awarded upon the following terms:

The award shall be for one year, but in the event of the holder of the scholarship showing exceptional ability he may be re-appointed.

The holder of the scholarship shall devote his time to original research in the Department of Pathology or of Physiology. He will, however, be expected to assist in the Laboratory, provided always that the amount of time required of him as such assistant demonstrator in the Laboratory shall not exceed four hours per week.

The award shall be made by a committee composed of the Professors of Physiology and Pathology and the Dean of the Faculty, who shall report as to the successful candidate after having given due attention to the results of the Annual Examinations and the character of the work done by him in the University Laboratories. The candidate selected shall be one who has during his undergraduate career given evidence of ability to pursue original research.

Applications for the scholarship must be sent to the Dean of the Faculty not later than the 15th of September, and the successful candidate shall begin work not later than the 1st of October, and shall devote at least eight months to the work.

The scholarship shall be paid in two instalments, half the amount on the 15th of October, and the other half on the 15th of January, provided the scholar gives evidence of having satisfactorily carried on the work up to that date.

The Starr Medals.

The late Richard Noble Starr, M.D., devised certain property for the encouragement of post-graduate study in Anatomy, Physiology and Pathology, and in fulfilment of this object one gold and two silver medals, called the "Starr Medals," are awarded annually to three candidates for the degree of M.D., who have shown by the theses which they have presented for that degree, that they have successfully pursued such study in any one of these subjects. The theses for which these medals are given must attain a standard approved of by the Board of Examiners, and the relative value of the theses will determine the rank of the candidates for the medals.

FEES FOR INSTRUCTION.

Registration (payable once only)....................$ 5 00
Tuition fees for the first year........................ 100 00
Tuition fees for the second year..................... 100 00
Tuition fees for the third year...................... 100 00
Tuition fees for the fourth year..................... 100 00
Tuition fees for the fifth year....................... 50 00
Tuition fee when repeating the year................. 25 00
Tuition fee for Graduates or Undergraduates in Natural
    Science Courses in Arts in first and second years.. 85 00
Biological laboratory supply fee in first year......... 2 00
Biological laboratory supply fee in second year....... 3 00
Physiological laboratory fee in first year............. 3 00
                                                       5 00

Special attention of the Students is called
that the Bursar's office hours are from 10 a.m.
Fees will in no case be received on Saturday
other days the regulation respecting the hours
will be strictly adhered to.

All fees are payable to the Bursar.

For Annual Examinations (each).................... ...
For Admission *ad eundem statum*.................... 10 00
For the Degree of M.B............................... 20 00
For the Degree of M.D............................... 20 00
For admission *ad eundem gradum*................... 20 00

The fee for examination, and, in the case of candidates of the Fourth Year, that for the degree, must be paid to the Bursar not later than the 20th March.

HOSPITAL FEES.

The Hospital fees—payable to the Hospital authorities—are as follows:—

Perpetual ticket................................$34 00
Annual ticket.................................... 14 00
Burnside Lying-in Hospital....................... 8 00

*NOTE: This fee is optional for students registered in the Faculty of Medicine prior to session 1905-1906.

to the results of the Annual Examinations and the character of the work done by him in the University Laboratories. The candidate selected shall be one who has during his undergraduate career given evidence of ability to pursue original research.

Applications for the scholarship must be sent to the Dean of the Faculty not later than the 15th of September, and the successful candidate shall begin work not later than the 1st of October, and shall devote at least eight months to the work.

The scholarship shall be paid in two instalments, half the amount on the 15th of October, and the other half on the 15th of January, provided the scholar gives evidence of having satisfactorily carried on the work up to that date.

The Starr Medals.

FEES FOR INSTRUCTION.

Registration (payable once only)....................$ 5 00
Tuition fees for the first year...................... 100 00
Tuition fees for the second year.................... 100 00
Tuition fees for the third year...................... 100 00
Tuition fees for the fourth year.................... 100 00
Tuition fees for the fifth year...................... 50 00
Tuition fee when repeating the year................. 25 00
Tuition fee for Graduates or Undergraduates in Natural
    Science Courses in Arts in first and second years.. 85 00
Biological laboratory supply fee in first year......... 2 00
Biological laboratory supply fee in second year....... 3 00
Physiological laboratory fee in first year............ 3 00
Physiological laboratory fee in second year........... 5 00
Chemical laboratory supply fee in first and second years. 3 00
*Library fee, payable in each year of undergraduate
    course...................................... 2 00

The annual fee for instruction in Medicine in each of the four years is $100 if paid on or before November 1st of the session. Arrangements may be made for deferring a portion of this sum. The terms may be learned upon application to the Bursar.

FEES FOR EXAMINATION AND DEGREES.

Students in the Fourth Year will be required, in addition, to pay a fee of $5 for the extra-mural class in Medical Psychology.

For Matriculation or Registration of Matriculation....$ 5 00
For Annual Examinations (each)................... 14 00
For Admission *ad eundem statum*.................... 10 00
For the Degree of M.B.............................. 20 00
For the Degree of M.D.............................. 20 00
For admission *ad eundem gradum*................... 20 00

The fee for examination, and, in the case of candidates of the Fourth Year, that for the degree, must be paid to the Bursar not later than the 20th March.

·HOSPITAL FEES.

The Hospital fees—payable to the Hospital authorities—are as follows:—

Perpetual ticket...................................$34 00
Annual ticket.................................... 14 00
Burnside Lying-in Hospital........................ 8 00

*NOTE: This fee is optional for students registered in the Faculty of Medicine prior to session 1905-1906.

MEDALLISTS.

Medicine.

g, gold medal; s, silver medal.

YR.
53 Oille, L. S., *g.*
  Aikins, M. H., *s.*
  Millar, T., *s.*
59 Barnhart, C. E., *g.*
  King, J., *s.*
  Francis, W. F., *s.*
60 Bascom, J., *g.*
  Playter, E., *s.*
  Tisdell, F. B., *s.*
  Morton, E. D., *s.*
  Ogden, W. W. *s*
  Martyn, D. H., *s.*
61 Hudson   *g.*
  Elliott, J, D., *s,*
62 Dolster, J., *g.*
  DeGrassi, G. P., *g.*
63 Ramsay, W. F., *g.*
64 McLaughlin, J. W., *g.*
65 Burnham, E. L., *g.*
  McCarthy, J. L. G., *s.*
  Kitchen, E. E., *s.*
66 Mickle, W. J., *g.*
  McCullough, J., *s.*
  Wadsworth, J. J., *s.*
67 Sparks, T., *s.*
  Palmer, R. N., *s.*
  Harbottle, R., *s.*
  Eccles, F. R., *s.*
  McFarlane, N., *s.*
  Nevton, J. H., *s.*
68 Brown, J. P., *g.*
  Hunt, R. H., *s.*
  Hove, T. C., *s.*
69 Graham, J. E., *g.*
  Humble, C., *s.*
  McCollum, J. H., *s.*
  Bentley, T. B., *s.*
70 Greenless, A., *g.*
  Burgess, T. J. W., *s.*
  Smith, C. M., *s.*
  Standish, J., *s.*
  Wagner, W. J., *s.*
  Burt, W., *s.*
70 Williams, A. D., *s.*
71 Forrest, W., *g.*
  Moore, C. Y., *s.*
  Henning, N. P., *s.*
  Delamater, R. H., *s.*
72 Zimmerman, R., *g.*
  Crozier, J. B., *s.*
73 Close, J. A., *g.*
  Beeman, M. I., *s.*
  Wright, A. H., *s.*
  Hagel, S. D., *s.*

YR.
74 Fraser, D. B., *g.*
  Brown, O. C., *s.*
  Farvell, A., *s.*
  Cameron, I. H., *s.*
  Shav, G., *s.*
  Fraser, D., *s.*
75 Britton, W., *g*
  White, J., *s.*
  Bennett, J. H., *s.*
  Eakins, J. E., *s.*
76 McPhedran, A., *g.*
  Lackner, H. G., *s.*
  Bowerman, A. C., *s.*
  Wilson, W. J., *s.*
77 Stuart, W. T., *g.*
  Orr, R. B., *s.*
  Richards, N. D., *s.*
78 Griffin, H. S. *g.* .
  Meek, H., *s.*
  Bonnar, J. D., *s.*
  Kennedy, G. A.,
  Gardiner, J. H., *s*
79 Burt, F., *g.*
  Mills, R. P., *s.*
  Chappell, W. F., *s*
80 Cross, W. J., *g.*
  Bryce, P. H., *s.*
  Ferguson, J., *s.*
81 Duncan, J. H., *g.*
82 Wallace, R. R., *g.*
  Duncan, J. T., *s.*
83 Robinson, W. J., *g.*
83 Dolsen, F. J., *g.*
84 Clerke, J. W., *g.*
85 Hovell, J. H., *g.*
  Carr, L., *s.*
85 Saunders, M. R., *s.*
  Hoople, H. N., *s.*
86 Peters, G. A., *g.*
  Noecker, C. T., *g,*
  Johnston, D. R., *s.*
87 Ego, A., *g.*
88 Féré, G. A., *g.*
  Gallovay, J., *s.*
89 Chambers, G., *g.*
  Collins, J. H., *s.*
  Godfrey, F. E., *s.*
90 Barker, L. F., *g.*
  Cullen, T. S., *s.*
  Philp, W. H., *s.*
  McFarlane, M. T., *s.*
  McGillivray, C. F., *s.*
91 Barnhart, W. N., *g.*
  Bollen, P., *s.*
  Boyd, G., *s.*
  McGorman, G., *s.*

YR.
92 Bruce, H. A., *g.*
  Middlebro, T. 11., *s.*
  Govland, R. H., *s.*
  Brovn, J. N. E., *s.*
93 Harvie, J. N., *g.*
  South, T. E., *s.*
  Elliott, W., *s.*
  Futcher, T. B. ⎫
  Harvey, E. E. ⎬ Æ, *s.*
94 McCollum, W. J., *g.*
  Rutledge, H. N., *s.*
  Crain, W. E., *s.*
  Johnston, H. A., *s.*
95 Merritt, A. K., *s.*
  McKay, T. W. G.
  McCrae, T., *s.*
  Hunter, A. J., *s.*
96 McCaig, A. S., *g.*
  Roberts, E. L., *g.*
  Graef, C., *s.*
  Goldie, W. S.
  Macklin, A. H., *s.*
97 Elliott, J. H., *g.*
  Hume, J. J. C., *s.*
  Nichol, R., *s.*
  Yeomans, W. L., *s.*
98 McCrae, J., *g.*
  Sutherland, G. A., *s.*
  White, W. C., *s.*
  Cahoon, F., *s.*
99 Wells, W., *g.*
  Hargrave, H. G., *s.*
  Piersol, W. H., *s.*
  Gow, J., *s.*
1900 P. L. Scott ⎫
  C. C. Bell ⎬ Æ, *g.*
  G.W.Howland ⎫
  D. G. Revell ⎬ Æ, *s.*
  E. D. Carder, *s.*
01 Clarkson, F. A., *g.*
  McIlwraith, D. G., *s.*
  Cleland, F. A., *s.*
  Carswell, W.A. ⎫
  Cohoe, B. A, ⎬ æq. *s.*
02 Roaf, H. E. ⎫
  Saunders, P.W ⎬ æq, *g.*
  Fletcher, G. W. *s.*
  Moir, A., *s.*
  Archer, A. E., *s.*
03 Oille, J. A., *g.*
  Phillips, J., *s.*
  Yin, S. C., *s.*
  Wilson, G. E. S., *s.*
04 McCulloch, R. J. P., *g.*
  Kinghorn, A., *s.*
  Anderson, R, W., *s.*
  Walker, S. B., *s.*

Starr Medallists.

67 Palmer, R. N.
63 Hunt, R. H.
  Brovn, J. P.
  Cassidy, J. J.
69 Graham, J. E.
70 Burgess, T. J. W., *g.*
  Greenless, A., *s.*
  Wagner, W. J., *s.*
71 Moore, C. Y., *g.*
  Henning, N. P., *s.*
  Forrest, W., *s.*
72 Zimmerman, R., *g.*
  Crozier, J. B., *s.*
73 Meldrum, N. W., *g.*
  Close, J. A., *s.*

74 Brovn, O. C., *g.*
  Farèvell, A., *s.*
  Campbell, A. J., *s.*
75 Britton, W., *g.*
  White, J., *s.*
  Bennett, J. H., *s.*
76 Lackner, H. G., *g.*
  McPhedran, A., *s.*
  Boverman, A. C., *s.*
77 Stuart, W. T., *g.*
78 Bonnar, H. A., *g.*
  Meek, H., *s.*
78 Griffin, H. S., *s.*
79 Burt, F., *g*
80 Cross, W. J., *g.*

  Bryce, P. H., *g.*
81 Duncan, J. H., *s.*
82 Wallace, R. R., *g.*
83 Robinson, W. J., *g.*
86 Peters, G. A., *g.*
89 Collins, J. H., *g.*
  Chambers, G., *s.*
90 Barker, L. F., *g.*
91 Barnhardt, W. N., *g.*
92 Middlebro, T. H., *g.*
  Bruce, H. A., *s.*
96 McKay, T. W. G., M.B.
  Rannie, J. A.
99 Hill, H. W.
1903 McCrae, T.

WINNERS OF FACULTY MEDALS AND SCHOLARSHIPS FOR 1905.

Medals.

Faculty Gold Medal.............................Lemon, W. S.
First Faculty Gold Medal........................Ford, G.
Second Faculty Silver Medal.....................Merritt, W. W. J.
Third Faculty Silver Medal......................Gowland, M. E.

Scholarships.

Second Year......................... { Gray, G. C.
 { Shier, W. C.

First Year.......................... { Harkness, J. G.
 { Davidson, R. E.

THE DANIEL CLARKE PRIZES IN MEDICAL PSYCHOLOGY.

1. Lemon, W. S.   2. Snelgrove, F. J.

POST-GRADUATE SCHOLARSHIPS.

THE GEORGE BROWN MEMORIAL SCHOLARSHIP IN MEDICAL SCIENCE.

Lemon, W. S.

STUDENTS OF THE UNIVERSITY FACULTY WHO RECEIVED THE DEGREES IN MEDICINE AT THE ANNUAL EXAMINATIONS OF 1905.

M.D.

Frederick James Brodie, M.B., 1904.
William Alexander Burr, M.B., 1904.
Herbert Eldon Roaf, M.B., 1902.

M.B.

William Henry Fitzgerald Addison, B.A., 1902
Elizabeth Catharine Bagshaw
Edith Beatty
James Campbell Beatty
George Isaac Black
Thomas Walter Blanshard
Richard Henry Bonnycastle
David H. Boddington
George Boyd
Samuel John Boyd
John Henry Richard Brodrecht
Frederick James Buller, B.A., 1901
Robert Bruce Burwell
Kelso C. Cairns
May Bernadetta Callaghan
Malcolm Hectorson Valentine Cameron

Walter Henderson Cameron
Francis Mervyn Campbell
James Alexander Campbell
Wellington Montelle Carrick
John Duncan Christie
Robert Leslie Clark
Herbert Burns Coleman
Thomas W. Collinson
Francis Herbert Coone
Howard Henry Gordon Coulthard
Harry Dalziel Cowper
James Malcolm Dalrymple
Sidney Raymond Dalrymple
Dingman Harold Williamson
Christian Benjamin Eckel
Wilfred George Evans
George Ford
Archibald John Gilchrist

William Carnochan Gilday
Edward Allan Goode
Marshall Edgeworth Gowland,
    B.A., 1901
Duncan Archibald Lamont Graham
George Wilbur Graham
Frederick W. Hall
Fred Vincent Hamlin
John Joseph Hamilton
Edward Charles Hanna
Ethelbert B. Hardy
Walter Sydney Laird
Lillian Carroll Langstaff
Willis Storrs Lemon
Granville Gordon Little
Roy Cathey Lowrey
Edwin James Lyon   .
Margaret McAlpine
Joseph McAndrew
Ernest Augustus McDonald
Fred. Fraser McEwen
John Aloysius McKenna
George Llewellyn McKinnon
Duncan Ferguson McLachlan
Garnet Douglas MacLean   ·
Charles McMane
Alfred McNally
Archibald George McPhedran, B.A.,
    1901
John Harris McPhedran
Thomas Thompson McRae
William Wingfield Medley
Willis Merritt
Edward Meredyth Middleton
James Irving Morris
Frederick Bruce Mowbray

Arthur Claude Munns
Charles Walker Murray.
William Joseph O'Hara
Charles Powell
William Ernest Procunier
James Alexander Rae
Hanna Emily Reid
Minerva Ellen Reid
William Roberts
Allison Montague Rolls
Charles Schlichter
John Archibald Scratch
Alexander Sinclair
Alexander Buchanan Smillie
William John Smith
Frederick James Snelgrove
John Hostley Soady
John Allen Speirs
Cecil Ellwood Spence
Alfred Howard Spohn
Charles Henry Stapleford
Alexander Porter Stewart
George Stewart
Victor Wellington Stewart
Arthur Washington Thomas
Robert Walter Tisdale .
James Harvey Todd
William Clare Toll
Seymour Traynor
Loftus Alex. Trueman
Frank Vanderlip
Arthur Gladstone Wallis
Frederick John Weidenhammer,
    B.A., 1896
James L. Wilson
Archibald Campbell Woods

CURRICULUM FOR THE DIPLOMA OF PUBLIC HEALTH.

1. The University shall offer a Diploma in Public Health (D.P.H.) on the conditions hereinafter detailed.

2. Candidates for the Diploma must be graduates in Medicine of this University, or of some other University recognized for this purpose by the Senate.

3. The curriculum leading to the Diploma shall extend over two Summer Sessions of three months each, and one Winter Session of six months.

4. The first Summer Session shall be devoted to Laboratory work in

    1. Sanitary Chemistry.

    2. Bacteriology.

    3. Parasitology.

5. The Winter Session shall be devoted to

    a. Advanced General Hygiene.

    b. Advanced General Pathology, including Theory of Immunity and Comparative Pathology.

    c. Elements of Geology, Meteorology and Climatology, in their relation to Public Health.

    d. Sanitary Engineering.

    e. Sanitary Legislation and Vital Statistics.

    f. Clinics on Contagious Diseases.

    g. History of Preventive Medicine and Epidemiology.

6. Candidates for the Degree of M.D. may substitute the foregoing Winter Course for such subjects or portion of subjects of the Fifth Year in Medicine as are not demanded by the College of Physicians and Surgeons of Ontario, at its final Examination.

7. The Second Summer Session shall be devoted to a course of Practical work in Public Health under the supervision of the Provincial Board of Health, including the methods of dealing with infectious diseases, inspection of schools and other public buildings, factories and dairies, inspection of water supplies and sewage disposal plants and other forms of municipal sanitation.

8. At the conclusion of the Winter Session an examination will be held on the subjects of the curriculum in Public Health specified in paragraphs 4 and 5, the passing of which shall be a necessary preliminary to entering upon the practical course indicated in paragraph 7.

9. Candidates who have passed the examination, and who present from the Provincial Board of Health a certificate of efficiency in the

subjects specified in paragraph 7, will be granted the Diploma of Public Health.

10. The fees for the Course shall be $150, payable in two instalments of $75 each at the beginning of the first Summer Session and the Winter Session respectively. The fee for the Diploma shall be $20.

11. Up to and including 1907, graduates in Medicine who have acted as Medical Health Officers for a period of two years may present themselves for the examination referred to in paragraph 8 without preliminary attendance on the Courses of Instruction. For such candidates the fee for the Diploma shall be $100.

CURRICULUM IN DENTISTRY.

DEGREE OF DOCTOR OF DENTAL SURGERY.

Matriculation.

Candidates for the degree of Doctor of Dental Surgery must pass the Matriculation examination hereinafter mentioned, unless

1. They possess a degree in Arts (not being an Honorary Degree), from some recognized University; or

2. Have already matriculated in the Faculty of Arts in this or some other University in Canada; or

3. Are Matriculants in the College of Physicians and Surgeons of Ontario; or

4. Have passed the Form III. or Form IV. Departmental Non-professional examinations in which the Latin option has been taken, it being understood that the equivalent examinations under titles no longer in force will be accepted.

Candidates not possessing any of the above named qualifications, will be required to pass the examination prescribed for matriculants in the Faculty of Arts in this University, provided always that candidates registered as matriculants of the Royal College of Dental Surgeons of Ontario, shall be admitted matriculants in the Department of Dentistry.

Candidates for the degree must matriculate before writing on any of the subjects prescribed for final examination.

Undergraduates.

Undergraduates (candidates for the degree), residents of the Province of Ontario, must have complied with all the requirements prescribed from time to time by the Board of Directors of the Royal College of Dental Surgeons of Ontario, for admission to examination for a certificate of license to practise Dentistry in Ontario.

Undergraduates (candidates for the degree), not resident in Ontario, must:

1. Have devoted at least three and one-half calendar years (not being engaged in any other business) to the study of Dentistry.

2. Must have attended at least three full courses of lectures, embracing all the subjects of the curriculum, of not less than seven months each, and including the daily clinic at a dental school recognized by this University; the last of which courses must be at the School of Dentistry of the Royal College of Dental Surgeons of Ontario.

3. Must have spent that portion of time, when not in attendance at lectures and clinics at the School of Dentistry, as students in the office of an approved dentist.

Examinations.

Candidates for the degree must pass two examinations, an intermediate and a final, an interval of not less than one year intervening between them. Until further provision be made, a certificate of having passed the intermediate examination of the Royal College of Dental Surgeons of Ontario will be accepted by this University.

Candidates for the final examination, which will be held at a time fixed by the Committee on Examinations, must present to the Registrar satisfactory certificates, covering all the requirements relating to undergraduates as given above, and of having passed the intermediate examination. The subjects for intermediate examinations shall be:—

(a) Comparative Dental Anatomy.
(b) General Histology.
(c) Bacteriology.
(d) Theory of Operative Dentistry.
(e) Theory of Dental Prosthetics.
(f) Dental Technique.
(g) Dental Materia Medica and Therapeutics.
(h) Principles and Practice of Medicine and Surgery as applied in Dentistry.
(i) Anatomy.
(k) Physiology.
(l) Chemistry.

The subjects for final examination shall be:—

(a) Theory and Practice of Operative Dentistry.
(b) Theory and Practice of Dental Prosthetics.
(c) Dental Pathology.
(d) Dental Histology.
(e) Principles and Practice of Medicine and Surgery as Applied in Dentistry.
(f) Dental Materia Medica and Therapeutics.
(g) General Anatomy and Special Anatomy of Head and Neck.
(h) Physiology.
(i) Chemistry.
(k) Jurisprudence.
(l) Orthodontia.

(These examinations will be written.)

(m) Practical Operative Dentistry.
(n) Practical Prosthetic Dentistry.

Candidates shall be examined in practical work from time to time, during the session of the Royal College of Dental Surgeons, on completion of the required work in the Infirmary and Laboratories of the College.

Annual examinations in April, and supplemental examinations in September, will be conducted under the joint auspices of the University and the Royal College of Dental Surgeons of Ontario.

Regular students of the Royal College of Dental Surgeons proceeding to the degree of D.D.S. may take the final examination in any subject at the close of the session in which it is completed in the College. The marks obtained in these subjects will be carried forward and tabulated with the results of the examinations of the final year.

No candidate shall be considered as having passed the examination who has not obtained 60 per cent. of the marks allotted; nor shall a candidate be considered as having passed in any subject who has not obtained at least 40 per cent. of the marks allotted to such subject.

Equivalent Examinations.

Examinations in the Faculty of Arts in the Department of Natural Science, Division 1, are accepted in lieu of examinations for the degree of Doctor of Dental Surgery, as follows:—

(a) Physiology and Chemistry of the Second Year for the Physiology and Chemistry of the intermediate examination.

(b) Histology of the Fourth Year for the General Histology and Bacteriology of the intermediate examination.

(c) Chemistry of the Third Year and Physiology of the Fourth Year for Chemistry and Physiology of the final examination.

(d) On application to the Senate, similar credits may be given for similar examinations passed in the Faculty of Arts or the Faculty of Medicine of other universities.

Fees.

The fee for examination for matriculation, in whole or in part, or for registration of any certificate accepted in lieu of examination, shall be five dollars.

The fee for final examination shall be ten dollars, which shall be paid before writing on any subject of the final examination.

The fee for supplemental examination in one or more of the final subjects shall be ten dollars.

The fee for the degree of D.D.S. shall be fifteen dollars, which shall be paid before writing on the examination of the final year.

No fee shall be charged for transference from any Faculty of the University to the Department of Dentistry.

The fee for admission *ad eundem gradum* shall be twenty dollars.

Concurrent Course in Medicine and Dentistry.

Students who are matriculants in the Faculty of Medicine and in the Department of Dentistry, may take a concurrent course in Medicine and Dentistry which will extend over six years.

Students taking this course will pass the regular University examinations in the subjects of the Medical curriculum from year to year as they are completed in the Medical Faculty, and in the final Dental subjects of the curriculum in Dentistry, from year to year as they are completed in the Royal College of Dental Surgeons.

Students taking this concurrent course, who have fulfilled all the requirements for the degree of M.B., and who have successfully passed the examination in the Dental subjects of the curriculum in Dentistry, including Dental Materia Medica and Therapeutics, shall receive the degree of D.D.S.

STUDENTS REGISTERED IN THE FACULTY OF MEDICINE, SESSION 1905-1906.

First Year.

Adams, F..........Detroit, Mich.
Adams, W. F. M.........Toronto
Anderson, G. W..........Toronto
Atkinson, C. F.......Tilsonburg
Baker, H. W............Toronto
Barrett, R..............Newton
Bayley, R..............Toronto
Belfie, G.............Gananoque
Bell, H..............Collingwood
Bernard, N. A.,
......Savanna-la-Mar, Jamaica
Boott, K.............Alvin, N.Y.
Boyd, J. S..............Simcoe
Brace, W. D..........Peterboro
Brandon, T. A...........Forest
Breuls, R. W...........Toronto
Bright, R. J. R.........Wiarton
Brown, A. G............Toronto
Bruce, H. H............Alliston
Brunet, E........Clarence Creek
Buckel, E. J............Toronto
Burnett, J. M.....Armstrong,B.C.
Campbell, D. A........Hepworth
Carnduff, J. M....Carnduff, Sask.
Christian, J. R..Edmonton, Alta.
Clarke, H. M...........Toronto
Collins, F. H..........Peterboro
Corrigall, J. W...Halbright, Sask.
Crawford, E. C. A.....Moorefield
Crews, W. H...........Trenton
Currey, D. V...........Toronto
Davis, R. E...............Ivy
Davis, R................Staffa
Davis, W..............Onandaga
Defries, W. J...........Toronto
Duck, J. A.............Lindsay
Duff, T. A. J.........Cookstown
Eacrett, E. J...........Exeter
Eager, J. C..........Waterdown
Earle, G. M...........Omemee
Ecclestone, W. M.......Toronto
Eedy, H. H...........Harriston
Ellis, S...............Windsor
Emerson, H. G........Wheatley
Emerson, P. J.....Victoria, B.C.
Ewens, H. B........Owen Sound
Eyres, H. H............Lindsay

Faris, M. N............Bradford
Faris, R. J............Bradford
Fish, E. S.....Humber Bay, P.O.
Forster, G. J.............Doon
Foster, A. H...........Windsor
Gardner, P. N..........Toronto
Gibson, J. R...........Millbank
Glionna, G. A. J........Toronto
Graham, J. L...........Ottawa
Guest, W. E...........Goderich
Gunn, G. C...........Seaforth
Hacquoil, A........Fort William
Haffey, M. J...........Toronto
Hall, H. C.Fort Qu'Appelle, Assa.
Hall, W...............Parkhill
Hannah, B.............Toronto
Harris, E. C.........Kingsville
Harvie, C. A............Orillia
Hauch, C. D..........Walkerton
Henderson, A. J..Wychwood Park
Henderson, E. K........Toronto
Hinds, F................Orillia
Holme, H. R........Oil Springs
Hopkins, B. H..........Lindsay
Hughes, C. A......Grenada, W.I.
Huxtable, E. W.......Sunderland
Irwin, O. M..............Lisle
James, G. W. S.....Bowmanville
Jamieson, W........Wellandport
Johnston, J. A.......Strongville
Johnston, H. Y..........Woburn
Kane, F. S...........Hamilton
Kells, G. W.......Palmerston
Kidd, G. C............Trenton
King, G. A.,
　　　New Westminster, B.C.
Lane, R. D...........Kinlough
Laurie, W. J...........Toronto
Leggett, W. G........Walkerton
Leighton, C. C.....St. Catharines
Lunz, G. J.............Drayton
Lynn, R. W............Warsaw
Macklim, J. E..........Toronto
Marcy, W. J. M.........Valens
Mavety, A. F....Toronto Junction
Miller, R. O...........Chatham
Mitchell, H. H.....Niagara Falls

10

Morgan, E...............Barrie
Moshier, H. H...........Sarnia
Murray, J. R. G........Toronto
Murray, K. M.........Woodstock
MacAlpine, C. D. H.....Lindsay
MacBeth, W. L. C.......Toronto
McBride, C. J...........Egbert
Macallum, A. B.........Toronto
McCaffrey, D..........:.....Madoc
McCort, E. A............Bolton
McCullough, W..L.....Hamilton
McDonald, M...........Sandfield
McEwen, S. F............Chesley
McEwen, R. J............Moffat
McInnis, J. A............Manilla
McIntosh, A. J..........:Toronto
McLaren, K. A..........Ottawa
McLean, W. T........Lucknow
McMaster, J. S..........Norwood
McPhee, J. D............Brechin
McQuade, E. A........Toronto
McQuade, G. C. A........Omemee
McTavish, H. R.........Palmyra
McTavish, R..........La Vallee
Naylor, A. E............Essex
Nelson, S. W. H.........Toronto
Nicholson, H. M.........Toronto
O'Connor, F. J......Campbellford
O'Neill, K. J............Arthur
Peart, T. W............Freeman
Pedlar, W. C............Uphill
Penny, W. G............Toronto
Pentecost, R. S.........Toronto
Philip, G. R............Hamilton
Pilcher, J. W........Owen Sound
Rae, E...............Burlington
Richards, J. N......Warkworth

Ritchie, A. B....Vergreville, Alta.
Robertson, A. G............:..Ivy
Robertson, F. N.......Walkerton
Robertson, L. B..........Toronto
Rogers, N. W.............Barrie
Sawdon, T...............Edgeley
Shaw, J. F...............Forest
Shields, H. J..........Mt.·Albert
Shields, H. A...........Brampton
Simpson, J. A...........:..Sarnia
Slater, W. D............Toronto
Smith, F. D,............Oshawa
Smith, R. A...........Roscomb
Solway, L. J...:.........Toronto
Spohn, P. D....Penetanguishene
Stephens, R. E.........Hamilton
Stevenson, W. O........Hamilton
Stone, J. G. R....Sault Ste. Marie
Sutton, A. E.........St. Thomas
Sweeney, J. B...........Arthur
Taylor, G. H.,
........Port of Spain, Trinidad
Telford, N................Valens
Terwillegar, N. L........Oshawa
Thomas, J...............Edgar
Thomas, R. H............Barrie
Thomas; W. M...........Birnam
Totton, C.....Wellman's Corners
Turrill, V. L............Aylmer
Tyerman, W. W.......Cranbrook
Tyrer, E. R.............Barrie
Waldron, C. W..........Toronto
Wells, E..R..............Barrie
Wesley, R. W.........Newmarket
Whetham, G. J.........Kirkwall
Wray, J. S.............Linwood
Yellowlees, N. J..........Toronto

Second Year.

Anderson, C. E.......Oil Springs
Armour, R. G..........Toronto
Backus, J. E............Toronto
Baldwin, St. G. P.......Toronto
Barnett, F. L..........Chippewa
Bates, H. K............Toronto
Beaver, G. W.....Lewiston, N.Y.
Boyd, E................Toronto
Bricker, J. G............Gorrie
Brown, A. H..........Stouffville
Brown, J. B.............Paisley
Brown, P. G............Toronto
Buswell, R. E........Centralia
Cairns, L. L..........Huntsville
Campbell, J. A.....Waubaushene
Carswell, D. F............Elora

Casserly, M. J.........Tottenham
Chapman, F. R............Essex
Clarke, D. W...-.....Ballyduff
Collins, A.........Niagara Falls
Collins, W. C.......Burin, Nfld.
Cottam, J. A.,
.New Amsterdam, Brit. Guiana
Coulter, W. G. G........Windsor
Craise, O. S.............Petrolia
Crassweller, H............Sarnia
Culham, H. A..........Hamilton
Daly, H. A...........Napanee
D'Arc, H. T............Toronto
Davidson, R. E........Beachburg
Davison, R. O...:.....Brantford
Day, W. E. C......Shallow Lake

Dorsey, C. F.........Collingwood
Edward, Miss M. L......Petrolea
Ellis, A. W. M.........Toronto
Elmore, C. W.........Springvale
Emmett, H. L..........Fonthill
Evans, A..............Virginia
Fader, W. R...........Windsor
Feldhans, H. W......Copper Cliff
Ferguson, A. D..........Fergus
Ferguson, W. D.........Valetta
Fielding, W. M.........Toronto
Fowler, J. M...........Petrolia
Fox, F. J...............Lucan
Francis, R. B...........Meaford
Galbraith, D. J.....Iona Station
Galbraith, J. L........Mt. Forest
Garrity, J. J...........Caledon
Gibb, W. B.........St. Mary's
Gideon, C. S.,
         Port Antonio, Jamaica
Glanfield, W. J.....Regina, Sask.
Graham, C. W.........Goderich
Green, T. M............Toronto
Grier, L. A. B.........Dundalk
Hamill, H. E..........Meaford
Hamilton, C. D........Cornwall
Hamilton, R. J.........Brinsley
Harkness, J. G..........Irena
Harrison, F. C.........Toronto
Harrison, J. P.......Dunnville
Harvie, W. A...........Orillia
Hawke, M. S...........Toronto
Haywood, A. K.........Toronto
Hewitt, C. D..........Toronto
Hill, C. E.............Toronto
Horton, B. B..........Actinolite
Hurst, R. L...........Freeborn
Hyland, G. H..........Toronto
James, A. B..........Brantford
Jamieson, D. B........Durham
Jamieson, D..........Glenarm
Jeffrey, E. S.........Toronto
Johnston, T. J........Carthage
Kelly, B. E........Bridgenorth
Keyes, J. E. L........Oakwood
Kinsey, A. L....:...Bracebridge
Krupp, W.........New Dundee
Lailey, W. W.........Toronto
Large, O. S............Poole
Lawson, J. H........Brampton
Leslie, N. V.........Hamilton
Linscott, G..........Brantford
Mabee, W.............Toronto
Mahood, C. S.........Lakelet
Marshall, J. F. S........Forest
Masten, R. C. D.......Toronto
Matthews, R. A. S......Toronto

Millar, A. H..........Castleton
Mills, S. G............Toronto
Millyard, W. S........Lucknow
Minthorn, H. L......Queenstown
Monkman, J. A....Stavely, Alta.
Montgomery, J. E........Barrie
Moore, H. H...........Weston
Moore, S. E...........Oliphant
Murray, A. M..........Newton
McCabe, L. G........Waterdown
McCormick, A. S.......Montreal
McCulloch, W. G.........Enfield
McEwen, J. A..........Hensall
Macfarlane, P. B........Toronto
McIlmoyle, W. D.....Fraserville
McKay, C. R.....Port Colborne
McKelvey, A. D.......Brussels
McKenzie, C. R......St. Thomas
MacKinnon, A. J......Star P.O.
McLean, J. E..........Orillia
McNiece, J. A.........Toronto
McPherson, J. L......Teeswater
Ogden, W. E...........Toronto
Paterson, R. H........Hamilton
Phair, J. T...........Toronto
Plewes, W. F..........Toronto
Pogue, O. A...........Lindsay
Powell, H. S.......Victoria, B.C
Pratt, W..............Cobourg
Prowd, C. W..........Desboro
Rice, A. G.....Toronto Junction
Ricker, A. C.........Dunnville
Richards, G. E........Newboro
Richardson, R. S.......Toronto
Roberts, M. C......Brigus, Nfld.
Robertson, W. A.......Monkton
Robertson, W. H.......Toronto
Rogers, G...........Kingsville
Ross, A..............Sarnia
Ross, W. C..........Peterboro
Ross, W. H..........Hamilton
Routledge, J. A.......Dunkeld
Rowland, C. E.........Toronto
Scott, H. B. E.......Listowel
Scott, W. R........St. Thomas
Sells, W. C......Niagara Falls
Sheard, R. H.........Toronto
Shepherd, W. G........Ottawa
Shepley, E.........Leamington
Smith, J. M........Cannington
Spencer, F. E.........Picton
Sproule, N. E. H.....Schomberg
Taylor, H. A......Wallaceburg
Taylor, N. B.........Toronto
Thompson, A. A.....Waterdown
Thompson, J..........Hastings
Tindale, W. E........Woodstock

Trow, E. J............Stratford
Tyerman, H. F.......Cranbrook
Verall, W. S..........Chatham
Walker, R. R........Waterdown
Wallace, A. H......Nelson, B.C.
Wallace, F. W.........Saintfield
Wallace, G. H..........Toronto
Weston, R. E. A.....Tilsonburg

Whiteway, C.,
........Musgrove Harbor, Nfld.
Wilford, E. C.............Blyth
Williams, G. W. ....Aurora
Willinsky, A. I.........Toronto
Wilson, F. D............Toronto
Worthington, G. H.......Guelph

Third Year.

Acheson, W. C........Mt. Healy
Adam, R. T.............Lindsay
Allison, D..............Belgrave
Anderson, J. S..........Wooler
Anderson, P. M........Belleville
Andrew, H. B..........Toronto
Baillie, W..............Toronto
Bates, G. A.............Toronto
Bell, H. W............Port Hope
Bennetto, F. R.......Palmerston
Bigham, J. F...........Culloden
Blanchard, E..........Leaskdale
Boyer, G. F..........Kincardine
Broddy, W. A..........Uxbridge
Broome, W. J..........Muncey
Brydon, W. H......Holly Park
Buck, G. S.............Lindsay
Burns, H. S..........Caledonia
Burns, J.............Palmerston
Callahan, T. H..........Wooler
Campbell, A. D.....Owen Sound
Cannon, O. A.............Vesta
Cerswell, B. S..........Toronto
Christie, J. G.........Duntroon
Cole, E. C.............Toronto
Crann, G. R.........Queensville
Crux, A.............Toronto
Dafoe, A. R............Madoc
Elliott, B. S..........Ingersoll
Evans, J. A............Islington
Faulds, R. W......Harrietsville
Fidlar, E..............Toronto
Field, J. J........New Liskeard
Fleming, A. G..........Toronto
Fowler, W. G........Teeswater
Gideon, E. D.,
........Port Antonio, Jamaica
Gillies, H..............Parkhill
Graham, E. V.........Bradford
Graham, L. B......Wallacetown
Graham, M...........Brucefield
Gray, G. C...........Waubuno
Harmer, C. G..........Toronto
Harrison, T. L.......Tilsonburg
Hartman, C. C.........Aurora

Hatcher, R. C....Bonavista, Nfld.
Hazelwood, J. F.Toronto Junction
Henderson, D. A.........Toronto
Henderson, E. M........Toronto
Hincks, C. M..........Toronto
Hunt, J. W.........Blind River
Huntsman, A. G........Toronto
Hurlburt, F. K....Manitowaning
Hutton, T. O.........Port Elgin
Jackson, G. P..........Toronto
James, H. J...........Toronto
Jamieson, C. V.........Guelph
Johnston, C..............Alma
Johnston, H. B......Vernonville
Johnston, H. W........Midland
Johnston, W. J........Wareham
Kakaza, T. M.,
......Port Elizabeth, S. Africa
Kay, A. F.............Virginia
Kenny, R. Y...........Sarnia
Ker, E. H. R......St. Catharines
Kirby, P. J.............Arthur
Knight, S. G.........Kincardine
Kyles, A. E...........Camilla
Lackner, H. M.. ......Berlin
Lapatnikoff, W.........Toronto
Large, W. B......Rochester, N.Y.
Leary, J. W. G.........Gormley
Leigh, S. S..........Hawkestone
Lipsitt, G. E........Mt. Brydges
Luckhoo, D. L.,
.New Amsterdam, Brit. Guiana
Middleton, F. C.........Woodhill
Miller, F. R............Toronto
Milne, J. D..........Delaware
Minns, F. S..........Woodstock
Mooney, C. N........Davenport
Morgan, H. A. E......Moorefield
Morrison, T...........Hamilton
Hulholland, R. P.......Toronto
McArthur, A. D......Greenbank
McClelland, W. A...Grand Valley
McCormack, V. W........Vivian
McCormack, W. G. M.....Vivian
McCutcheon, R. H......Nobleton

McFadden, H. M........Millbank
MacKay, J. T...........Toronto
MacKenzie, D. W........Toronto
MacKenzie, K. N.....St. Thomas
MacLachlan, J...........Toronto
McLean, A. A...........Clachan
Macleod, J. A.........Priceville
McLeod, N.........Moose Creek
McNichol, O. A....Pittsburg, Pa.
McPhedran, W. F........Toronto
McPherson, A. W........Toronto
McPherson, G. A.....St. Thomas
McRuer, J. M...............Ayr
McVicar, C. S........Ailsa Craig
Naismith, A. G.........Milverton
Newell, O. J............Aylmer
Nickle, M. A.............Madoc
Norman, T. H.........Schomberg
Orr, T. S..............Hamilton
Platt, E. O............Plainfield
Prentice, A. J...........Drumbo
Quarry, J. J...........Centralia
Racey, G. W.........Kirktown
Reid, P................,.Erin
Relyea, E. H...........Cornwall
Richardson, E. F........Aurora
Ritchie, L. W.........Beamsville
Robb, J. O............Ilderton
Robertson, D. E........Toronto
Ross, G. W............Burford
Ross, H. R............Burford
Routley, F. W..........Toronto

Ryckman, W. C......Burlington
Savage, J. P..........Brantford
Scheck, W. S..........Hamilton
Schinbein, A. B........Listowel
Shier, W. C...........Uxbridge
Simpson, L. J.........Thornton
Siung, S. H.,
.New Amsterdam, Brit. Guiana
Sparks, G. L..........St. Mary's
Speers, J. H............Toronto
Sproat, J...........Nelson, B.C.
Stewart, R.............Bluevale
Stinson, S.............Brighton
Sutherland, J. W........London
Taylor, W. A...Toronto Junction
Thompson, C. P........Listowel
Thompson, J. J..Toronto Junction
Towers, T. L.............Sarnia
Tye, P. L............Goderich
Walker, H.......Stockton, Cal.
Walsh, W. C..........Millbrook
Whillans, D. W........Ilderton
Whillans, J. A.........Ilderton
White, S. T..........Shelburne
Whitmore, G. H.Toronto Junction
Williams, D. A........Allenford
Willson, H. G..........Toronto
Wilson, C. E..........Napanee
Wilson, N. K..........Toronto
Woods, H. B.............Belfast
Young, E. H............Guelph

Fourth Year.

Balfour, D. C.........Hamilton
Bethune, W...........Hamilton
Black, D..............Toronto
Blair, J. K............Tarbert
Bowman, F. B..........Dundas
Browne, W. E.........Midland
Bryans, W. E........Jamestown
Calhoun, J. C..........Toronto
Campbell, A. A.....Shanty Bay
Campbell, K.......Bruce Mines
Cartwright, V. E......Aldershot
Chapin, C. G.........Waterford
Cleaver, E. E..........Toronto
Coghlan, R. O.......Wyoming
Colwill, R.............Vasey
Cooper, G.........Gravenhurst
Counter, J. W..........Toronto
Courtice, J. T.........Castleton
Crookshank, J. G......Blenheim
Cumming, C. R...........Galt
Dawson, F. B..Maple Creek, Alta.

Dickson, E. C............Orillia
Dillane, R. H.......Tottenham
Douglas, F. A..........Toronto
Duncan, J..............Toronto
Edwards, R. G.........Hornby
Ellis, T. A...........Kingscote
Frawley, N. D..........Orillia
Galloway, H. H.....Oxbow, Alta.
Gardiner, G. H.......Mt. Forest
George, E............Port Elgin
Gillis, E. D..........Muirkirk
Graham, M. R......Wallacetown
Hawkins, C. S..........Canton
Heatlie, N. J............Solina
Henderson, A.........Palmerston
Henderson, M. S..St. Paul, Minn.
Hodgson, E. G..........Toronto
Holbrook, J. H.........Toronto
Holmes, J. M..........Chatham
Honey, W. B.,
. ....Savanna-la-Mar, Jamaica

Houston, G. W...........Tweed
Howard, E. A. E... .Hagersville
Howes, D. E......Drew Station
Huehnergard, H..........Berlin
Humphries, R. E........Walton
Hutton, R. L.........Brantford
Jackson, J. H.............Eckel
Jessop, E. T.............Fergus
Johnston, R. M.Grassie's Corners
Jones, R. A..........Mt. Forest
Kaufmann, W. P.,
      Georgetown, Brit. Guiana
Kaufman, V. S.........Chesley
Kemp, H. W. S.........Maxwell
Kendall, W. B..........Toronto
Kenrick, M. A..........Comber
Kilgour, D. M..........Guelph
Kirkpatrick, C. G....Oro Station
Lang, O. K.............Granton
Langmaid, C. A.....Bowmanville
Lewis, W. A.............Barrie
Lindsay, H. J. R.....St. Thomas
Loudon, J. D...........Toronto
Madden, E. J...........Stayner
Magwood, J. S. N.......Lindsay
Main, L...............Sheffield
Malcolm, G. G......Shanty Bay
Mann, R. W........Bridgenorth
Manning, F. W.........Windsor
Mason, V. A....Marshfield, Wis.
Masson, J. C...........Toronto
Mayhood, F. H.....Calgary, Alta.
Mitchell, A...........Hamilton
Monkman, H. S.........Watford
Moorhead, A. S........Toronto
Munn, F. J............Toronto
Munro, N. A.........St. Thomas
Murray, D. A.........Underwood
McCannel, A. D..........Chesley
McClure, W. A.......Woodbridge
McCormick, W. J......Belleville
MacIntyre, G. C......St. Mary's
Macintyre, R. W.......Toronto
McKee, J. F............Toronto

McKenzie, D...........Brussels
MacKinnon, M. A......Copleston
McLean, A. B..........Stayner
Maclean, H...........Copleston
McMillan, R. J..........Dutton
McNeil, H. M..........Toronto
Ochs, W. H...........Hespeler
Organ, F. W.........Waterdown
Overend, S. A........Caledonia
Pain, A..............Hamilton
Phillips, A. C..........Toronto
Pratt, W. C...........Petrolea
Rankin, A. B..........Toronto
Reid, W. H...........Lucknow
Rich, W. T...........Oakwood
Ripley, A. T........Wallacetown
Robert, J. X..........Chatham
Rolph, A. H...........Toronto
Royce, H. T.........Davenport
Ruby, R. H......New Hamburg
Russell, J. D...........Acton
Shaw, R. N.......Niagara Falls
Sheridan, W. J..........Merton
Slemon, C. W...........Haydon
Smale, R. R........Bowmanville
Spence, J...........Webbwood
Sproule, W. B.........Thornton
Sproule, W. J. D.....Schomberg
Stewart, H. A........St. Thomas
Stipe, R...............Toronto
Stobie, R. H.........Desbarats
Storry, J. H..........Mt. Albert
Swain, W. W......Grand Valley
Taylor, E. C...........Hanover
Thibeaudeau, A. A....Chatham
Thompson, H...........Watford
Thornton, F. B........Consecon
Thrush, C. A. M..........Byng
Vernon, F. G..........Uxbridge
Weldon, T. C...........Toronto
Williams, R. A........Ingersoll
Wodehouse, R. E......Blenheim
Woodhall, F...........Hamilton

Fifth Year.

Bell, L. J., M.D.........Chesley
Bell, N. J., M..B.Toronto Junction
Blanchard, T. W., M.B...Appleby
Bloom, W. D., M.D., C.M.Toronto
Boddington, D. H., M.B.,
      ....Leamington

Burgess, H. W., M.D., C.M.
      ....Toronto
Coulthard, H. H. G., M.B.,
      ....Toronto
Moran, S. A., M.B...Rednersville.
Paulin, S., M.B..........Toronto
Sloane, J. G., M.B.....Toronto

Occasional Students.

Bancroft, L. . . . . . . .Vankleek Hill
Black, W. A. . . . . . .Pugwash, N.S.
Blair, J. F. . . . . .London
Bleakley, J. A. . . . . .Kemptville
Billings, M. R. . . . . .Lyn
Brooks, C. E. . . . . .Woodstock
Chalmers, W. L. . . . .Vankleek Hill
Cheney, H. L. . . . . . .Vankleek Hill
Clapperson, S. . . . . .Hamilton
Dalrymple, W. A. . . . . . .Bismarck
Duffin; D. W. . . . . .Belleville
Grainger, J. W. . . . . .Walkerton
Hamilton, R. . . . . .Gorrie
Higginson, T. D. . . . .Hawkesbury
Johnson, A. L. . . . . .Strathroy
Lane, C. . . . . .Goderich
Little, C. R. . . . . .Chatham
Mathieson, W. A. . . . . .Toronto
Mills, L. I. . . . . .Fergus
Morrow, H. M. . . . . .Omagh

McGuirl, W. H. . . . . .Ottawa
MacKenzie, A. . . . . .Toronto
McKeown, G. H. . . . . .Russell
McLachlan, C. C. . . . . .Renfrew
Nott, B. F. O. . . . . .Oshawa
O'Neill, J. G. . . . . .Arnprior
Pettigrew, J. D. . . . . .Norwood
Pollock, F. . . . . .Kincardine
Ramore, W. D. . . . . .Fergus
Reid, H. W. . . . . .Toronto
Rickard, H. B. . . . . . .Bowmanville
Roberts, J. G. . . . . .Toronto
Somers, C. . . . . .Toronto
Steele, G. J. . . . . .Toronto
Stewart, J. . . . . .Ruthven
Thompson, J. E. . . . . . .Sunderland
Vosper, L. . . . . .Campbellford
Wickinson, H. G. . . . . .Stratford
Wurts, W. B. . . . . .Stouffville

Summary:

First Year Students.   165

Second Year Students.   158

Third Year Students.   149

Fourth Year Students.   127

Fifth Year Students.   10

Occasional Students.   39

Total.   648

CPSIA information can be obtained
at www.ICGtesting.com
Printed in the USA
BVHW041035210219
540828BV00009B/462/P

9 781397 327765